ID665927

AROUND **atlanta** WITH *KIDS*

CREDITS

Writer: Mary Jo DiLonardo

Series Editors: Karen Cure, Andrea Lehman
Editor: Christina Knight
Editorial Production: Ira-Neil Dittersdorf
Production/Manufacturing: Angela L. McLean

Design: Fabrizio La Rocca, *creative director;*
Tigist Getachew, *art director*
Illustration and Series Design: Rico Lins, Keren Ora
Admoni/Rico Lins Studio

ABOUT THE WRITER

Mary Jo DiLonardo, a contributing writer for *Atlanta* magazine for five years, has been to every kid-related attraction in town—both in the line of duty and for the enjoyment of her 5-year-old son, Luke. She has also written for *The Atlanta Journal-Constitution* and the Atlanta-based CNN.com.

FODOR'S AROUND ATLANTA WITH KIDS

Copyright © 2003 by Fodors LLC

Fodor's is a registered trademark of Random House, Inc. All rights reserved under International and Pan-American Copyright Conventions. Published in the United States by Fodor's Travel Publications, a unit of Fodors LLC, a subsidiary of Random House, Inc., and simultaneously in Canada by Random House of Canada Limited, Toronto. Distributed by Random House, Inc., New York.

No illustrations or other portions of this book may be reproduced in any form without written permission from the publisher.

First Edition
ISBN 1-4000-1164-7
ISSN 1541-3179

IMPORTANT TIP

Although all prices, opening times, and other details in this book are based on information supplied to us at press time, changes occur all the time in the travel world, and Fodor's cannot accept responsibility for facts that become outdated or for inadvertent errors or omissions. So always confirm information when it matters, especially if you're making a detour to visit a specific place.

SPECIAL SALES

Fodor's Travel Publications are available at special discounts for bulk purchases for sales promotions or premiums. Special editions, including personalized covers, excerpts of existing guides, and corporate imprints, can be created in large quantities for special needs. For more information, contact your local bookseller or Special Markets, Fodor's Travel Publications, 1745 Broadway, New York, NY 10019. Inquiries from Canada should be directed to your local Canadian bookseller or sent to Random House of Canada, Ltd., Marketing Dept., 2775 Matheson Boulevard East, Mississauga, Ontario L4W 4P7. Inquiries from the United Kingdom should be sent to Fodor's Travel Publications, 20 Vauxhall Bridge Road, London, England SW1V 2SA.

PRINTED IN THE UNITED STATES OF AMERICA
10 9 8 7 6 5 4 3 2 1

AROUND atlanta WITH KIDS

by Mary Jo DiLonardo

Fodor's Travel Publications
New York • Toronto • London • Sydney • Auckland

www.fodors.com

COUNTDOWN TO GOOD TIMES!

Extra! Extra!

High Fives

Something for Everyone

All Around Town

Many Thanks!

GET READY, GET SET!

Everyone knows that organizing a family's schedule is a full-time job. Pickups, drop-offs, school, parties, after-school activities—everyone off in a different direction. It's an organizer's dream, but a scheduling nightmare. Spending time together shouldn't be another thing to have to figure out.

We know what's it's like to try to find good places to take your children or grandchildren. Sometimes it's tough to change plans when you suddenly hear about a kid-friendly event; besides, a lot of those events end up being crowded or, worse, sold out. It's also hard to remember places you read about in a newspaper or magazine, and sometimes just as difficult to tell from the description what age group they're geared to. There's nothing like bringing a "grown-up" 12-year-old to an activity that's intended for his 6-year-old sister. Of course, if you're visiting Atlanta, it's even more challenging to figure out the best things to do with your kids before you even get there. That's where we come in.

What you'll find in this book are 60 ways to have a terrific couple of hours or an entire day, with children in tow. We've scoured the city, digging out activities your kids will love—from circling the hulking dinosaurs at Fernbank Museum of Natural History to learning about the Civil War in-the-round at Atlanta Cyclorama. The best part is that it's stress-free, uncomplicated, and easy for you. Open the book to any page and find a helpful description of a kid-friendly attraction, with age ratings to make sure it's right for your family, smart tips on visiting so that you can get the most out of your time there, and family-friendly eats nearby. The address, telephone number, open hours, and admission prices are all there for your convenience. We've done the work, so you don't have to.

Naturally you'll still want to keep an eye out for seasonal events that fit your family's interests—from festivals and parades to arts events and free concerts. Welcome spring at the Conyers Cherry Blossom Festival in March, then celebrate again in April at Piedmont Park's Dogwood Festival, Atlanta's oldest event. In May check out the jam-packed Music Midtown festival. Join the city's Fourth of July traditions by lining up to cheer the Peachtree Road Race, the world's largest 10K run, or watch the Salute 2 America 4th of July parade, perhaps the largest Independence Day parade in the country. If your popsicle-stick projects need inspiration, head to September's Yellow Daisy Festival in Stone Mountain, one of the country's top arts and crafts shows. Nearly every little town in the suburbs and beyond has an annual event—from the Prater's Mill Country

Fair in Dalton to arts festivals on the square in Marietta and Roswell. Centennial Olympic Park has plenty of spring and summer family days filled with entertainment and music, and by spring 2003, the Children's Museum of Atlanta will have opened next door to the park.

WAYS TO SAVE MONEY

We list only regular adult, student, and kids' prices; children under the ages specified are free. It always pays to ask at the ticket booth whether any discounts are offered for a particular status or affiliation (but don't forget to bring your I.D.). Discounts are often available for senior citizens, AAA members, military personnel, and veterans, among others. Many attractions offer family memberships, generally good for one year of unlimited use for your family. These memberships sometimes allow you to bring a guest. Prices vary, but the memberships often pay for themselves if you visit the attraction several times a year. Sometimes there are other perks: newsletters or magazines, members-only previews, and discounts at a gift shop, for parking, or for birthday parties or special events. If you like a place when you visit, you can sometimes apply the value of your one-day admission to a membership if you do it before you leave.

Look for coupons—which can often save you $2–$3 per person—everywhere from the local newspaper to a supermarket display. The Atlanta Convention & Visitors Bureau has ticket packages (www.atlanta.net/packages) which cover admission to attractions such as Zoo Atlanta, Six Flags, World of Coca-Cola, and Stone Mountain. But unless you spend the discount coupons you get for shopping at CNN Center and Underground Atlanta, the savings are minimal—in some cases only a couple dollars. You can, however, get same-day half-price tickets to theater, dance, music, and other performances, including the Center for Puppetry Arts, by visiting the AtlanTIX booth at Underground Atlanta. (Check out www.atlantatheatres.org or call 678/318–1400 to see what's available.)

WHEN TO GO

With the exception of seasonal attractions, kid-oriented destinations are generally busiest when children are out of school—especially weekends, holidays, and summer—but not necessarily. Attractions that draw school trips can be swamped with clusters of sometimes-inconsiderate children tall enough to block the view of your preschooler. But school groups tend to leave by early afternoon, so weekdays after 2 during the school year can be an excellent time to visit museums and zoos. For outdoor attractions, it's good to visit after a rain, since crowds will likely have cleared out.

The hours we list are the basic hours, not necessarily those applicable on holidays. Some attractions are closed when schools are closed, but others add extra hours on these days. It's always best to check if you want to see an attraction on a holiday.

SAFETY

Obviously the amount of vigilance necessary will depend on the attraction and the ages of your kids. In crowded attractions, keep an eye on your children at all times, as their ages warrant. When you arrive, point out what the staff or security people are wearing, and find a very visible landmark to use as a meeting place, should you get separated. If you do split into groups, pick a time to meet. This will decrease waiting time, help you and your kids get the most out of your time there, and manage everyone's expectations.

FINAL THOUGHTS

Actually, this time it's yours, not ours. We'd love to hear what you or your kids thought about the attractions you visited. Or if you happened upon a place that you think warrants inclusion, by all means, send it along, so the next family can enjoy Atlanta even more. You can e-mail us at editors@fodors.com (specify the name of the book on the subject line), or write to us at Fodor's Around Atlanta with Kids, 1745 Broadway, New York, NY 10019. We'll put your ideas to good use. In the meantime, have fun!

—Mary Jo DiLonardo

ALLIANCE THEATRE FAMILY SERIES

Atlanta's premier resident theater has been staging successful plays since 1968 and is the largest regional theater in the southeast. The same talented group of actors who appear in the Alliance's regular season also perform in the annual family series that includes two shows for kids, as well as the beloved annual production of "A Christmas Carol."

Accommodating youthful attention spans, the two kids' shows are an hour long each with no intermission. Avid readers will recognize many of the show's titles—performances have included *The Hobbit*, *Charlotte's Web*, *James and the Giant Peach*, and *Lilly's Purple Plastic Purse*. After the curtain goes down each Saturday and Sunday, members of the cast return to the stage for a chat with the audience. Kids can ask questions—everything from "how long does it take to memorize your lines?" to "where do you change costumes?"

Although not specifically a children's show, *A Christmas Carol* attracts many families. The two-hour performance is broken up by one fifteen-minute break. Sometimes there's a pre-

EATS FOR KIDS Within walking distance to all three theaters is the food court at the Colony Square Mall (1197 Peachtree St.) next to the Sheraton hotel. The culinary selections are as diverse as Chinese, Italian, Middle Eastern, and French. There are sandwiches and lots of tempting baked goods at **Corner Bakery Café** (1201 Peachtree St., tel. 404/817–7111). Next door at **Houlihan's** (1197 Peachtree St., tel. 404/873–1119) you can dine on pot roast, ribs, or sandwiches while the kids choose from mac 'n' cheese, corndogs, and pizza.

 Venues include Alliance Stage,
Woodruff Arts Center,
1280 Peachtree St., Midtown

 Tickets $12.50–$42

 Oct–Mar, dates and times vary

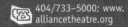 404/733-5000; www.
alliancetheatre.org

 5 and up

show discussion with cast members about the show and its author, Charles Dickens. Because the tale's ghosts might scare the teeniest tots, the age recommendation is five and up.

Most shows appeal to older preschoolers and up, but some are targeted toward middle school children. If you're in doubt, call the Alliance Theatre (tel. 404/733-4650) to find out the actual content of the play (themes, language, etc.) and ask for what ages the piece is appropriate. At least one of the children's plays each season is held on the Alliance Stage. The other shows alternate between the nearby 14th Street Playhouse and the adjoining Hertz Stage. Dress is casual at all three venues. Applause is highly recommended.

HEY KIDS! How fast can you change your clothes? In a musical production, the actors have usually 60 seconds or less to make a costume change. Plus they get changed in the dark backstage with little or no privacy. At least you can lock the bathroom door!

KEEP IN MIND Every year the Alliance Theatre sponsors a special family fun day at Woodruff Arts Center. Usually held in conjunction with one of the season's children's plays, "Families Center Stage" is an entire afternoon filled with entertainment, crafts, and workshops related to the subject of the play. Tickets are generally a few dollars more than regular performances and include food, the actual performance of the play, and even a show by a wacky marching band. The event is for kids (and adults) of all ages.

AMERICAN ADVENTURES

Not every little kid is ready to tackle mile-high roller coasters and other scary amusement park rides, so American Adventures created a scaled-down alternative specifically for the pre-teen set. However, the white-knuckle ride of choice is still a roller coaster. It's much smaller than those at American Adventures' sister park, Six Flags Over Georgia, but it has some pretty daunting ups and downs from a kid's eye-view. Older thrill-seekers choose the coaster, the bumper cars, and the Tilt-A-Whirl, while the little guys are quite happy lining up for the soaring swings and the choo-choo train.

A chain of five semi trucks chugs around a track with their horns honking. Next door, a fleet of airplanes soars in circles eight feet off the ground. Across the way, teacups twirl and hot air balloons go up, up and away, their baskets full of screaming youngsters.

Of the park's 14 rides, only about half appeal to preschoolers. That makes a visit pretty pricey for the pre-K set. There are minimum height requirements on many of the rides

HEY, KIDS!
If you've never driven a go-cart, you may want to try your hand at the NASCAR-style stock cars ($5). You must be over 58" tall to drive alone but if you're at least 40" you can take the wheel as long as there's an adult with you.

KEEP IN MIND
Until noon every day, the rides are opened in rotation, so only half of them are operating during any given time. All the rides are up and running in the afternoon. And be aware, you have to buy your tickets inside the arcade building at the park's entrance. That means your kids will have to walk by all sorts of beckoning arcade games (four tokens for a dollar). If you have another adult in your party, you may want to have the kids wait outside with him or her while you buy tickets in order to avoid the temptation.

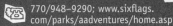 250 Cobb Pkwy., Marietta

770/948–9290; www.sixflags.
com/parks/aadventures/home.asp

 $5 adults (accompanied by child), $15 children over 36", $5 children under 36"

June–mid-Aug, 10–8; Mar–May and mid-Aug–Sept, weekends, times vary

Ages 3 to 8

so that the bravest toddlers couldn't climb aboard even if they wanted to. On some attractions little ones can ride as long as a parent tags along.

When the sun gets too hot (or the lines get too long), head indoors to the Foam Factory, a three-story playground filled with scads of colorful foam balls. Kids run around, scooping up the balls in vacuums and hurling them across the room. The whole scene is loud and chaotic with kids climbing rope ladders and swooshing down slides.

Back outside, duffers make their way through the park's miniature golf course, complete with a waterfall, a big ship, and a talking robotic dock master who collects balls at the end of the round. Like the rest of the park, the course shows signs of wear and tear, but the giggling youngsters don't seem to mind.

EATS FOR KIDS You can eat inside next to the Foam Factory at the **Inventor's Club**. They serve pizza and chicken tenders as well as a kid's meal complete with peanut butter and jelly, chips, and juice. There's also a nearby concession stand that sells snacks and drinks. For more fun, less than a mile down the road is the famed **Big Chicken** (12 Cobb Pkwy., tel. 770/422–4716), a Kentucky Fried Chicken restaurant starring a four-story chicken with rolling eyes and a yellow beak that opens and shuts. In addition to chicken, you'll find souvenirs like Big Chicken key chains and T-shirts.

AMICALOLA FALLS STATE PARK

Amicalola Falls is probably metro Atlanta's most awesome natural attraction. At 729 feet, it's the tallest waterfall east of the Rocky Mountains. It may be big, but you really have to work hard to see it.

With no effort whatsoever, you can drive to the very top of the waterfall and look down. It's pretty, but to get the full breathtaking impact, you have to start at the bottom and work your way up. After a .3-mile hike up a fairly strenuous and often steep dirt path, you'll come to the first overlook, where oohing and ahhing compete with the roar of an incredible wall of water racing down humongous rocks. A metal stairway leading up from here makes the remaining ascent a bit easier.

If you're feeling adventurous (and your kids are at least 4–5 years old) climb 176 steps up to the bridge that spans the towering cascade. (It's 704 steps to the very top—somewhere

EATS FOR KIDS Picnic tables and shelters are all over the park, including at the top of and near the bottom of the falls. You can buy snacks at the visitor's center, but the only restaurant within the park is the Amicalola Lodge's **Maple Restaurant** (tel. 706/265–8888). It offers a mountain view and standard breakfast, lunch, and dinner buffets (free for kids 3 and under). All sorts of restaurants line the square in the lovely town of Dahlonega, 15 miles (20 minutes) away. (*See* Crisson Gold Mine and Funky Chicken Art Project.)

 Hwy. 52, Dawsonville

 Free ($2 parking)

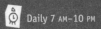 Daily 7 AM–10 PM

 800/573-9656; http://ngeorgia.com/
parks/amicalola.html

 4 and up

around 60 stories high.) Reach your hands out to feel the spray as water rushes all around you. Underfoot, you can see the water streaming wildly through the metal slat floor.

This unbridled torrent of Mother Nature wows most kids. But it's the adults, not the children, who often complain about the climb. It's not stroller-friendly, and you sure don't want to take toddlers who have to be carried. But the creek across from the visitor's center is perfect for wading, the water is only knee-deep, and there are turtles, frogs, and tadpoles waiting to be discovered.

The bulk of the park's 1,021 acres are wild, crossed by a handful of beautiful trails. Most are at least moderately strenuous. Some family-friendly options are the Lodge Loop, a .4-mile gravel trail near the lodge, and the mile-long Day Use trail from the visitor's center to the pond.

HEY, KIDS! Wanna go fishing? You can borrow a fishing pole and tackle for free at the visitor's center then head down to Reflection Pond at the base of the falls. Even if you don't catch any trout, it's fun to watch all the tadpoles swimming around.

KEEP IN MIND Although black bears, coyotes, and bobcats live in the park, chances are you won't see them unless you're there really early in the morning or at dusk. If you want to see wildlife from a safe distance, stop in the visitor's center (open daily 9–5). A couple of (stuffed) black bears are on display, as well as quite a few live non-venomous snakes—like the colorful red and gold corn snake curled up in an old farm boot. The box turtles are harmless, too.

ANDRETTI SPEED LAB

A trip to Andretti Speed Lab calls for lots of bravery and lots of cash. Kids—who must be at least eight years old *and* at least 48" tall—zip around a racetrack at speeds as fast as 45 miles per hour. Parents wince as the kids zoom past each other on twisted curves, motors roaring, hands gripped to the steering wheels. What seems like an eternity ends in six minutes—somewhere around 15–20 laps. When the racing heat ends and the parents are through biting their fingernails, the speed demons stride out triumphantly clutching their sleek black helmets and trying hard not to lose their cool by grinning too widely. Andretti is a young thrill seeker's paradise.

Kids under 16 get their own track so don't worry about your child sharing the road with hot-rodding adults. All racers don helmets and bright blue and green jumpsuits and are required to watch a short video that explains the rules and how to drive the race carts. It's pretty self-explanatory—the red pedal is the brake, the green one is the gas—so it's not too tough for kids to grasp. But be prepared, the track attendants admit that,

HEY, KIDS!

Before racing, you should know what it means when the track attendant waves a flag. Green means go. Yellow means slow down. Blue means move over. Red means stop. If you see a black flag, you're out of luck. It means your race is over.

EATS FOR KIDS You can dine on burgers at **Fuddruckers** (tel. 678/352–3290) right inside the building. Kid's meals (which include fries, drink, and a cookie) offer a choice of hot dog, grilled cheese, hamburger, or chicken tenders. To get away from the racecar noise, head a couple blocks south to **Dreamland BBQ** (10730 Alpharetta Hwy., tel. 678/352–7999) where the kids can marvel at the barbecue pit right there in full view. For south of the border instead of just plain south, try **El Mexica Gourmet** (11060 Alpharetta Hwy., tel. 770/594–8674). Its walls are hung with colorful piñatas, lights, and sombreros.

on the junior track, "kids are crashing all the time." No one gets hurt, courtesy of the seatbelt and the padded helmets—but it's not for the faint of heart.

If you have last-minute doubts, have the kids test their mettle on the climbing wall instead, where they also must be at least 8 and 48". After being harnessed to a safe belay system, they scramble up the side of the 40-foot wall by grabbing blue and green rubber handholds as they go. In the next room, young daredevils strap themselves into the zip line, an apparatus that sends them shooting across the room on a suspended wire, courtesy of gravity.

Through it all, you can hear the coursing vroom-vroom of the speeding cars and the pounding of hip music as you empty your wallet and work on that ulcer.

KEEP IN MIND Besides racing, rock climbing, and the zip line, there's tabletop shuffleboard and billiards ($10/hour). There are also dozens of blinking and buzzing video arcade games ranging from a quarter to $2 per play. Be aware, however, that there's not much there for the little siblings who are too young to race. Most of the games require a lot of skill or are too violent for young children. The exceptions are an updated skeeball game and air hockey tables. Prize tickets can be redeemed for penny candy and small toys.

ATLANTA BALLET'S NUTCRACKER

One of Atlanta's longest-standing holiday traditions is Atlanta Ballet's presentation of the classic tale, the *Nutcracker*. Performed by the company since the 1960s, this version is an elaborate spectacle filled with everything from flying sleighs and exploding cannons to falling snow and dancers floating in midair. Each year thousands of kids fill the audiences at The Fox Theatre while 300 local children get to don costumes and perform.

The fairytale story revolves around a little girl named Marya who gets a soldier-like nutcracker toy for Christmas. She falls asleep under the tree and dreams that the nutcracker comes to life, saving her from a platoon of rats. When the nutcracker wins the battle, he turns into a prince and joins Marya on a trip from the land of snow to the kingdom of sweets where they meet the Dew Drop Fairy.

If your children have never seen a live performance before, this fun and fanciful show is a good place to start. There's so much activity and excitement on stage, it should keep

HEY, KIDS! The dancers may make those leaps and twirls look easy, but they've been practicing for years to get their moves just right. If you think dancing takes a lot of energy, here's a little *Nutcracker* trivia by the numbers. Every performance of the Atlanta Ballet's *Nutcracker* uses 300,000 watts of electricity—enough to light up an entire football stadium! Also during each and every show, twenty pounds of artificial snow falls, and the Christmas tree on stage grows three stories, from 13 feet to 38 feet tall. Although the Nutcracker's mask looks really heavy, it's actually made of foam and weighs only two pounds.

The Fox Theatre,
660 Peachtree St., Midtown

 Tickets $20–$60

 Dec., dates vary

 Ticketmaster 404/817–8700;
www.atlantaballet.com

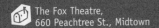 4 and up

the attention of even preschoolers for the entire two hours. Even the fight between the rats and toy soldiers is less menacing than buffoonish. They tease and torment each other, all the while moonwalking and doing silly stunts. The good guys, of course, win. There's one 15-minute intermission and plenty of snacks like popcorn and candy at the concession stands.

The Fox is an attention-grabbing theater itself. Before the show and at intermission, Christmas carols are played on the theater's famous organ, Mighty Moe. The elaborate stage and curtains are incredibly ornate and look like something out of an Arabian fairy tale. Make sure your kids put their heads back and look up at the domed ceiling covered with hundreds of sparkling stars and floating clouds.

KEEP IN MIND
Got a budding star on your hands? Atlanta Ballet holds *Nutcracker* auditions each year in September for children age 10 through 18. Kids should have gymnastic or dance experience in order to be considered for one of the hundreds of on-stage roles. Call 404/873–5811 for details.

EATS FOR KIDS Three blocks east is the Atlanta institution **Mary Mac's Tea Room** (224 Ponce de Leon Ave., tel. 404/876–1800). There's grilled cheese, chicken tenders, and macaroni and cheese on the "mini-mac" menu. Three blocks south is the **Gordon Biersch Brewery & Restaurant** (848 Peachtree St., tel. 404/870–0805), a lively spot with kid-friendly eats like pizza, ravioli, hamburgers, and grilled cheese. Just one block from The Fox, **Gina's Italian Restaurant** (710 Peachtree St., tel. 404/875–4019) has pizza-by-the-slice.

ATLANTA BOTANICAL GARDEN

This garden isn't just silver bells and cockle shells and pretty flowers planted all in a row, but a fun-filled educational exploration of Mother Nature. The first thing that grabs kids' attention in the Children's Garden is the gaping mouth of a googly-eyed, six-foot high caterpillar, into which kids quickly disappear. With flower-topped antennae, purple eyelashes and a welcoming smile, the critter is far from scary. He's the opening spot for the maze of hedges that shows—through pictures, explanations, and silly fun—how caterpillars make their transformation into beautiful butterflies. After navigating the maze, kids run under a striped canopy representing the cocoon-like chrysalis, through butterfly-shaped doors, and into a butterfly garden. And that's just the first stop.

Aimed at kids 4 to 11, the Children's Garden really appeals to even younger (but not much older) budding naturalists. It's two acres of hands-on experimentation where kids can do cool things like touch a Venus flytrap (you *can* stick your finger in, but if you use a skinny twig instead, the plant's creepy "jaws" can clamp shut completely). All the neat

KEEP IN MIND Family programs are held in the outdoor amphitheater in the Children's Garden on Saturday mornings April through July, and September through early November. Presentations range from African dance to storytelling with plants. Check the Web site or call the Garden for schedules.

HEY, KIDS! Outside the Children's Garden, check out the conservatory's three terrariums filled with tiny poison dart frogs. You won't have to search too hard for the brilliantly colored creatures that come in vivid yellow, blue, and orange. In the wild, those bright colors warn predators to stay away or risk the consequences! Listen closely and maybe you can hear their high-pitched singing. There are even some escapees hopping around inside the conservatory. But don't panic. Thanks to their regulated diets, they're no longer poisonous.

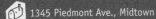 1345 Piedmont Ave., Midtown

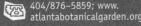 404/876–5859; www. atlantabotanicalgarden.org

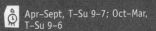 $10 adults, $5 students (with any school ID), children under 3 free; Free Th 3–7PM

 Apr–Sept, T–Su 9–7; Oct–Mar, T–Su 9–6

8 and under

stuff here is pint-sized. Adults have to go through a boring gate while kids get to stoop underneath a hole in the fence. They can hide in a giant watering can, climb through a gigantic plant stem, and walk behind a waterfall.

On a path between two kiddie prerequisites—a dinosaur garden (sift through sand to find plant fossils) and a playground— is a lesson in bee behavior. How does a bee tell the rest of her colony where the good flowers are? She does a dance. Kids can do the dance themselves with help from the stone markers outside the working beehive. Take two steps here, spin around there, and in no time they're doing the bee waggle dance.

The whole Children's Garden is stroller-friendly with restrooms conveniently tucked behind the limestone "green man" (half-plant, half-human) fountain. There's another fountain for splashing and lots of shaded benches for parents who want to sit back and watch future horticulturists (and lawn-mowers) cultivate those little green thumbs.

EATS FOR KIDS Right outside the bridge to the Children's Garden there's **The North Courtyard**, a spot for sandwiches and cookies. Outside the Garden, there isn't much kid-friendly fare within walking distance (and parking is always a problem in adjacent Piedmont Park). Head to the opposite end of the park to **Woody's Famous Philadelphia Cheesesteaks** (981 Monroe Dr., tel. 404/876–1939) for hotdogs and sandwiches. If the line is too long, try **Fabiano's Italian Delicatessen** (985 Monroe Dr., tel. 404/875–0500), where hoagies and ready-made, neatly packaged sandwiches await you.

ATLANTA CYCLORAMA

Atlanta is rife with history, and it's harder to find a denser concentration of it than at the Cyclorama. The Civil War—specifically the Battle of Atlanta in July 1864—comes to life via the world's largest oil painting. Sound boring? It's not.

The painting is an impressive 42 feet high and more than 350 feet wide (it would cover roughly the same area as two football fields). It's part of a multi-dimensional, theater-in-the-round experience. You climb up a wall of stadium-like seating, which rotates as a voice-over narrates the battle's history before you. The painting is accompanied by a diorama—a 3D scene complete with soldiers, covered wagons, and landscape. It's nearly impossible to tell where the scene ends and the painting begins.

After the first rotation, you'll take one more lap around the painting, this time with a helpful narration from one of the Cyclorama volunteers. You'll find out all sorts of interesting facts such as its weight (nearly 9,000 pounds), its creation (in 1886) and amusing trivia. (Look

KEEP IN MIND When you enter the actual Cyclorama after watching the introductory film, hike up the steps toward the top of the theater. The higher you go, the better the view of the panoramic circular painting and the overall experience. For kids, there's nothing frightening about the actual experience (the bank of seats move but very slowly) but be aware that the lights stay dim when you're entering and leaving the theater in order to make a breathtaking impression when the program first starts.

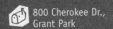 800 Cherokee Dr., Grant Park

 404/658-7625; www.bcaatlanta.org

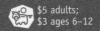 $5 adults; $3 ages 6–12

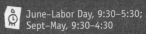 June–Labor Day, 9:30–5:30; Sept–May, 9:30–4:30

 6 and up

for a soldier resembling Clark Gable and the painted horse with no legs thanks to hungry rats.)

The Cyclorama experience is preceded by a short film that sets the stage by describing the events leading up to the Battle of Atlanta. Obviously, it's tough to depict war without guns, bloodshed, and dying. So make sure your child is mature enough to handle the experience.

Afterwards, head upstairs to the Civil War Museum to see a cannon and caisson, all sorts of revolvers and muskets, uniforms, canteens, and cavalry boots.

It's tough to miss, but be sure to check out the locomotive in the lobby. *The Texas* was used in the Great Locomotive Chase of 1862. In that battle, at least, the Confederates— and the train—won.

EATS FOR KIDS
There's no food in the building but the Cyclorama is smack dab in the middle of historic **Grant Park**, right next to Zoo Atlanta. There are plenty of tables, benches, and lots of lawn space perfect for a picnic lunch on the park's 127 acres. Too bad you can't get Civil War action figures at the **McDonald's** (800 Cherokee Ave., tel. 404/622–4482) right outside the Cyclorama.

HEY KIDS! See all those soldier figures surrounding the Cyclorama? There are 128 of them posed in the landscape surrounding the painting. They look life-size but they're actually a lot smaller than they appear. The soldiers range in size from 11 inches to 42 inches (which is only 3½ feet tall.) They used to be standing in real red clay with real branches and trees, but the clay got dusty and the trees encouraged rats and pests to move in. Now all the "nature" you see is made of fiberglass and plastic!

ATLANTA HISTORY CENTER

K ids often give text-heavy documents and relics entombed in glass the fly-by treatment, so the Atlanta History Center waves them down with "please touch" signs, interactive exhibits, and displays that invite comparison and analysis. Representing the area's history and the Civil War are folk art works that can be handled, multimedia exhibits with computer stations, and even historic buildings that have been moved to the museum's property.

Preschoolers and kids up to about age six can play in an 1894 shotgun house (a shot fired through the front door would've gone right out the back), make pretend calls on an 1890 telephone, and crank the handles on the photo viewers to look at old pictures of Atlanta. There's a comfortable alcove where they can listen to animated recordings of ghost stories and tall tales from around the time of the Civil War.

Authentic cannons, uniforms, an army wagon, and flags in the Civil War exhibit, "The Turning Point," might inspire junior high schoolers' history homework. Videos, computer

HEY, KIDS!
Feel like going on a treasure hunt? Ask at the front desk for a family guide for one of the exhibits. You'll get a handful of clues to solve a historical puzzle. Look for the magnifying glass logo as you explore the exhibit.

EATS FOR KIDS
The Coca-Cola Café in the center's lower level is set up like a 1950s soda fountain shop, complete with floats and milk shakes, as well as hot dogs, grilled cheese, and sandwiches. If you don't mind a two-block walk, **Henri's Bakery** (61 Irby Ave., tel. 404/237–0202) has sandwiches and a monstrous array of cookies, doughnuts, and muffins. A couple of doors down at **The Rib Ranch** (25 Irby Ave., tel. 404/233–7644) there's barbecue fixins' and fun walls covered with license plates, saddles, and autographed dollar bills.

 130 W. Paces Ferry Rd., Buckhead

 $12 adults, $7 children 4–17, children under 4 free

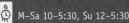 M–Sa 10–5:30, Su 12–5:30

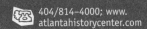 404/814-4000; www. atlantahistorycenter.com

 3 and up

stations, and maps aid in describing the progress of the war, but side-by-side placements of guns and a battlefield amputation kit aptly reveal the realities of a soldier's life.

To demonstrate work skills once common in the area, costumed docents carve furniture from tree stumps or hand-pick cottonseeds from recently harvested cotton at the center's mid-19th century Tullie Smith Farm (Sept–May, T–Th 10–12:30). Tours of the house are continuous but what may grab kids' attention more is petting the sheep or watching the chickens strut around outside.

Although the Swan House, a 1928 mansion, is also open for tours, it's filled with decidedly non-kid-friendly fancy furnishings. So let them play outside; there's a huge front lawn where they're welcome to run around. The gardens in the back have trails and a hidden elephant statue perfect for climbing. The Victorian playhouse is off-limits, but there's not a single breakable item inside the 1937 playhouse behind the museum.

KEEP IN MIND The Atlanta History Center holds special programs throughout the year for families and children. On a Saturday in April, sheep are sheared and their wool is washed, dyed, and woven into a spring shawl on Sheep to Shawl Day. Magic Monday programs for toddlers and preschoolers have crafts, storytelling, and music, and the first Sunday of each month at Tullie Smith Farm brings demonstrations of bee keeping, candle dipping, basket-making, and woodworking.

ATLANTA ROCKS!

I f your kids are always scampering up trees, crawling to the top of the jungle gym, or scaling fences, let them climb to their hearts' content at the largest indoor climbing gym in the southeast. The 12,000-square-foot facility is lined with 25-foot high walls and some towering boulders for your little ones to tackle with their best Spider-Man moves.

First-timers should sign up for a Novice Climb. You'll spend two hours in the gym with other new climbers under the supervision of staff (the ratio is six climbers to one staff person). It's not an actual instructional class where you learn how to belay, but you will get help when you need it and some general how-to climbing tips.

There are 50 ropes (called top-rope stations) that hang from the top of the walls. Each rope has three different climbing routes distinguished by color-coded hand and foot holds on the wall. You can choose the green path or the orange route but most kids tend to do "rainbow climbing." They just grab whatever holds they can reach as they clamber to the top.

EATS FOR KIDS There are many dining options less than a quarter mile up the road at the corner of Collier and Howell Mill. Get sandwiches, salads, and cookies at **Home-spun Café** (2020 Howell Mill Rd., tel. 404/352–4120) or grab juice, bagels, and danishes next door at **Joe Muggs** (2020 Howell Mill Rd., tel. 404/350–0461). You can get Atlanta's best-known pizza at **Fellini's** (1991 Howell Mill Rd., tel. 404/352–0799). "Standard bur-ritos" at the popular **Burrito Art** (1950 Howell Mill Rd., tel. 404/425–0030) include pulled pork and Asian meatloaf.

  1019-A Collier Rd., next to Collier Industrial Park, Buckhead

404/351–3009; www.atlantarocks.com

 $23 two-hour novice climb; daily rates for belay-qualified $13.50 M–F, $15.50 Sa–Su

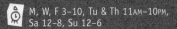 M, W, F 3–10, Tu & Th 11AM–10PM, Sa 12–8, Su 12–6

6 and up

If your kids know what they're doing, they have to pass a one-time belay check ($3) to show that they know how to use the equipment. Those that pass the test pay less expensive daily climbing rates or can buy a membership. There are also introduction-to-climbing classes ($35) for kids 12 and up, where they'll learn everything from how to belay to the correct way to wear a harness.

It's best to dress in loose fitting, cotton clothes like knee-length shorts and T-shirts. Nylon clothing, like soccer shorts, tends to bunch up and become uncomfortable under the climbing harness. Wear sneakers or any comfortable closed-toe shoes, or you can rent special climbing shoes ($3.75; free with novice climb.) There's no minimum age but most climbers are at least 5 years old. Spider-Man pajamas are optional.

KEEP IN MIND
If you don't want to go downtown, there's a smaller Atlanta Rocks! in Doraville (4411-A Bankers Circle, tel. 770/242–7625) that has 6,500 square feet of climbing surface with 40 rope stations. (M & F 6PM–10PM, Tu–Th 3–10, Sa 12–8, Su 12–6.)

HEY KIDS! Falling is highly unlikely thanks to all the safety harnesses and ropes. But just to be on the safe side, the gym floor is covered seven or eight inches deep with black and blue spongy rubber chips. The material is actually shredded sneaker rubber from Converse, the same company that makes athletic shoes. Although it's tempting to throw the rubbery stuff at each other, one of the gym rules is no playing with the flooring chunks. There's also no running and no swinging like Tarzan from the ropes.

BELLSOUTH TELEPHONE MUSEUM

I n a world of cell phones, touch-tone, caller ID, and speed-dial, this museum is history's wake-up call to 21st-century kids who only might have to ask for their parents' permission, not for an operator's assistance, to make a phone call.

Among the signs and photos showing the evolution of Alexander Graham Bell's first telephone in 1876 into today's communications technology, you'll find trivia like the fact that Bell insisted the phone be answered "Ahoy" because he didn't like "Hello." Your kids will no doubt head for the interactive exhibits like the authentic 1924 Model-T Ford truck in the middle of the museum. Press the green button and the truck shakes and makes revving sounds before launching into a monologue about how telephone service employees have battled everything from fires to storms while restoring phone service to their customers. Right around the corner, two 1930s era phones are just asking to be touched. Let your

HEY KIDS!

If the telephone's inventor, Alexander Graham Bell, had known his words would be part of history, he may have said something a little more interesting to his assistant than, "Mr. Watson, come here. I want you" the first time he spoke into his groundbreaking invention!

EATS FOR KIDS There are fast food restaurants throughout BellSouth Center and plenty of tables and chairs in the atrium. At **Pacific Grill** (tel. 404/876–1122), on the lower level, you'll find Asian meals of tofu, vegetables, shrimp, and chicken. Next door, **Café du Jour** (tel. 404/876–8133) has roll-up sandwiches, baked potatoes, salads, and chicken. There are also a couple of delicatessens, a Mexican restaurant, and a doughnut shop in the building. For more famous fare, the well-known **Varsity** (61 North Ave., tel. 404/881–1706) is just a couple of blocks away.

BellSouth Center,
675 W. Peachtree St., Midtown

404/529-0971;
www.bellsouthgapioneers.org/
Museumtemp.htm

 Free

 M–F 11–1

 4 and up

kids pick up one of the phones and start dialing numbers. The wall of switching equipment behind them clicks and moves, showing the complicated process involved in making just one phone call.

Ahead are even more buttons surrounding a map of metro Atlanta. Press the blue button and blue lights start blinking, showing cellular service throughout the city. Press purple and you'll see mobile data service. Green shows the fiber optic network and orange denotes paging service. When all the buttons are pressed, the map twinkles like a Christmas tree. Throughout the museum are dozens of mostly original and some replica phones dating from 1876 through the 1970s. Interesting models include the bulky field phone used in World War II, the dial-less phones from the early '30s that contacted the operator to make connections, and a 1969 picture phone that was extolled as the phone of the future.

KEEP IN MIND It's best to make a reservation to see the museum a couple of days in advance of your visit. That way you can have a free, guided tour, and you won't have any difficulties getting in. If you just arrive during the museum's hours of operation without a scheduled tour, there's a chance it won't be open. If that's the case, go to the security desk downstairs and ask to be let in.

BIG TREES FOREST PRESERVE

Tucked amid the car dealerships, businesses, and residential neighborhoods of Sandy Springs is this 30-acre urban forest where you won't see baseball diamonds, picnic tables, or Frisbee golf. The land was purchased by a land trust to save it from development, and the undisturbed wooded oasis is meant only for quiet walks and nature observation.

Pack binoculars if you have them, park in the Fulton County North Annex Building lot, and then take to the trails that pass towering white oaks, creeks, bridges, and stunning overlooks. The 350-foot paved entrance trail is the most stroller-friendly. The rest of the trails are covered with a dense blanket of soft wood chips. The terrain is mostly easy but there are some slightly steep climbs and uneven (yet fun) creek crossings where you have to walk across big flat rocks.

If it weren't for the occasional traffic sounds from Roswell Road, the forest would have the feel of a far-off oasis. There are hardly any manmade items intruding here. Seats are made

KEEP IN MIND If you like what you see at Big Trees, drive two miles to the **Albert Schweitzer Nature Preserve** (455 Abernathy Rd.), behind the Georgia Veterinary Specialists emergency clinic. The preserve, an outreach project of the Big Trees Forest, encompasses five acres with a half-mile walking trail, bridges, creeks, waterfalls, and swings (of the porch, not playground, variety). It's open free to the public from sunrise to sunset. The trails are covered in wood chips, and in some places there are sharp drop-offs, so hang on tight to the little ones.

from century-old fallen oaks, trail signs are unobtrusive wood markers, bridges are built of stones and wooden planks. Some 1,400 volunteers including Eagle Scouts, school groups, and garden clubs work to keep the preserve pristine, carting wood chips, clearing fallen trees, and shoring up the creek banks.

A self-guided nature trail teaches children about preservation without being preachy. You can learn how parking lots flush debris into nature, how a natural spring sustains plants and creatures, and why fallen trees help preserve the environment. At the end of their hikes, kids can write in the park's comment book about their experience in nature.

Just remember to read the extensive list of rules at the trail entrance. If your kids can keep from running, yelling, and traipsing off the trails, Mother Nature (quietly) awaits.

HEY, KIDS! Sure, you see birds like red-tailed hawks and blue herons as well as squirrels when you're wandering around Big Trees, but look closer. The preserve is home to at least two families of red foxes who have dens inside old logs. In the creek, look for tadpoles, salamanders, fish, and frogs.

EATS FOR KIDS As long as you promise to clean up after yourself, you're welcome to brownbag it and eat in the preserve. Unpack your fixings at a scenic area on the lower trail that's surrounded by oak-stump seats and big flat rocks overlooking the streams. Outside the preserve, you can dig into fried chicken, meatloaf, and homemade breads at **Grammy's Buffet** (7878 Roswell Rd., tel. 770/698–8413), which also has an irresistible dessert bar. Or indulge in the all-you-can-eat pizza buffet at **Cici's Pizza** (6690 Roswell Rd., tel. 404/257–9944) where kids 3 and under eat free.

For more than a decade, Burt's Farm has been *the* place to go for pumpkins. Among the thousands the Burt family sells each fall, you'll find jack-o-lanterns-to-be tipping the scale at 100 pounds—the record-holder weighed in at 235 pounds. The ones that wouldn't even fit into your trunk make for great photos with gap-toothed kids grinning beside them.

The Burts harvest 110 acres of gourds and pumpkins and 60 acres of popcorn and Indian corn each year. The crops—divided by size, shape, and type—are then spread out in huge fields at the front of the farm. Grab a wheelbarrow and let the kids comb the brilliant orange rows in search of their perfect pumpkin. Prices range from 75 cents (for small decorative gourds in wild colors and unusual shapes) to as much as $75 for huge pumpkins that could make squash out of most preschoolers.

KEEP IN MIND To make your pumpkin last longer, follow a few simple guidelines. Never buy a pumpkin for carving if it has any soft spots. Handle your pumpkin as little as possible so it doesn't get bruised. When you get it home keep it in a cool, dry place. Once you carve it, most pumpkins only last four or five days before getting soft and rotting.

EATS FOR KIDS There are always homegrown snacks for sale at Burt's including popcorn balls, slices of pumpkin pie, caramel corn, and pumpkin muffins. On weekends a concession stand sells hot dogs, nachos, and soft drinks. For something more substantial, go less than a mile west down the road (left out of the farm) to **Under the Hemlock** (Hwy. 52 and Hemlock Dr., tel. 706/265–4603) for sandwiches and snacks. In the other direction, about a mile east at Amicalola Falls State Park, the **Maple Restaurant** (Hwy. 52, tel. 706/265–8888) in the lodge has basic breakfast, lunch, and dinner buffets (free for kids 3 and under).

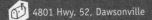  4801 Hwy. 52, Dawsonville

 Hayrides $4
ages 13 and up,
$3 ages 2–12

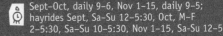 Sept–Oct, daily 9–6, Nov 1–15, daily 9–5;
hayrides Sept, Sa–Su 12–5:30, Oct, M–F
2–5:30, Sa–Su 10–5:30, Nov 1–15, Sa–Su 12–5

800/600–BURT;
www.burtsfarm.com

 2–11

After securing your find, take a hayride (wear long pants because you'll be knee-deep in straw). The 20-minute trek on a tractor-pulled covered flatbed rambles through corn fields, pumpkin patches, and across a covered bridge. Along the way you'll pass mechanical bluegrass pickers singing a song and two "talking" pumpkins.

When the farm opens September 1, the crowds are at their slimmest. Things get much more hectic the closer it gets to Halloween, but that's when the most pumpkins are harvested and when the selection is the greatest. Inside the big red barn at the farm's entrance you can stock up on all kinds of Halloween supplies. There are pumpkin carving and painting kits, special jack-o-lantern candles, and pumpkin face stickers (if you want to avoid carving altogether).

HEY, KIDS! If you go on the hayride, take a close look as the tractor pulls you through the cornfields. See those flattened areas where it looks like somebody smashed all the corn stalks and had a party? They most certainly did! The black bears that live in the surrounding woods like to come out at night and help themselves to fresh corn on the cob. They don't clean up after themselves too well. Fortunately, they usually leave the pumpkins alone unless they're really hungry!

CAGLE'S DAIRY

After a trip to Cagle's Dairy, your children will never look at a glass of milk the same way again. This Canton farm—the only remaining dairy in Georgia that produces and processes its own milk—offers an up close and personal look at the whole milk-making procedure from what goes in (the feed) to what comes out (the milk).

Start by clambering aboard a hay wagon that rumbles its way through a leisurely tour of the farm. As the wagon passes silos, the feed yard, and grazing cattle, your helpful guide (sure to be an actual Cagle) points out the finer points of dairy farming while passing around cottonseed, molasses, and other things cows eat. When your wagon enters a pasture of expectant bovine mothers, the farm's star Border collie quickly rounds them up and marches them toward the wagon. Strategically placed feed buckets encourage them to come up close for a face-to-face encounter.

Kids get to watch as a calf is bottle-fed, impressively gulping down a half-gallon of milk in just under two minutes. They get to feed greens to the calves and are then herded off

EATS FOR KIDS Take your packed lunch and free Cagle's milk across the road to the farm's designated picnic area, complete with lots of green grass, a covered area, and plenty of restrooms, soap, and water. For authentic Southern country fare, chow down on mac and cheese, meatloaf, or fried chicken at **Family Traditions** (6321 Hickory Flat Hwy., tel. 770/345–7117) or the barbecue a couple of miles down the road at **Pappy Red's B-B-Que** (13670 Arnold Mill Rd., tel. 770/475–9910). The pocket PB&J sandwiches are guaranteed kid-pleasers and the pig decor should keep little ones highly entertained.

 362 Stringer Rd., Canton

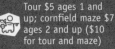 Tour $5 ages 1 and up; cornfield maze $7 ages 2 and up ($10 for tour and maze)

 Tour days and times vary; by reservation only. Cornfield maze Sept–mid-Nov, Th–Su

 770/345-5591 or 770/704-5713 for recorded information; www.caglesdairy.com

 2 and up

themselves to watch Miss Rosie, an amiable heifer, get milked. There's a stop in the processing room where the milk is pasteurized, homogenized, and bottled, a walk through the cooler, then a complimentary half-pint of Cagle's own white or chocolate milk as a souvenir. On Cagle's fall harvest tours you can buy your Halloween pumpkins after a hayride. Instead of milk, you'll get a free baby pumpkin when you leave.

The dairy looks, feels, and *smells* like a real farm because it is. Twice a day (2:30 AM and 2:30 PM) some 100 or so of the cows get milked. That's why the farm is usually only open to the public in the morning. It's a rare opportunity for city-slickers to get a taste—literally and figuratively—of real old-fashioned farm life. Just watch where your step!

KEEP IN MIND
During the school year, family days are set aside once or twice a week while the rest of the time is reserved for school groups. If you call ahead, you can sometimes join a school group tour. Family days are more frequent in summer. The detailed schedule is online and available by calling the farm.

HEY KIDS! If you head to the dairy in the fall, get lost in the cornfield—on purpose! Every September, the Cagles hire a maze designer to cut patterns in their seven-acre cornfield. Then they give you a riddle card filled with clues so you can try to work your way out of it. It is possible to navigate the twists and turns in only 15 minutes but your card's puzzling mystery could keep you wandering in the maize maze for an hour! If you run into a cow, you know you're heading in the wrong direction.

CENTENNIAL OLYMPIC PARK

An awful lot of squealing and giggling goes on at Centennial Olympic Park. In the summer, children gleefully dart through the spray and spurting jets of the Fountain of Rings—a great way to dodge the sweltering temps. In winter, the 85,000 lights and dozens of intricate light displays of "Holiday in Lights" earn exclamations of delight.

Year-round all eyes are on the fountain when show time is announced. Kids scamper out of the water and jump on the surrounding walls to get the best view as the water jets shut down. When the first few notes of Neil Diamond's "Coming to America" kick in, the water starts to dance in a synchronized 20-minute program set to music. In between songs, a taped announcement offers park trivia tidbits (there's more pneumatic tubing and wiring in the park than in a Boeing 747 jet, for example). The highlight is the final number, the upbeat "Under the Sea" from Walt Disney's "The Little Mermaid," when the

HEY, KIDS!
The Fountain of Rings is made up of 251 water jets, 400 fog jets, and 487 lights (colored clear, amber, and red). About 5,000 gallons of water recycle through the fountain each minute. That's enough to fill an average backyard swimming pool in five minutes!

KEEP IN MIND Among the park's many scheduled events are free summer concerts on Friday night and on Tuesday and Thursday afternoons. But the park's Family Fun Days with themes such as sports, the great outdoors, and cultural arts are a can't-miss for kids. April through September, on the fourth Saturday of the month from 12–4, the free event features street performers, entertainment, arts and crafts projects, and food. Local performing arts organizations and museums, such as the Atlanta Ballet and SciTrek, participate.

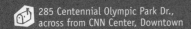
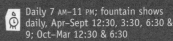

water sprays go as high as 35 feet. For the twilight and evening shows, lights flash along with the music.

A legacy of the 1996 Olympic games, the 21-acre park includes a large playground at its north end and a "Quilt of Nations" pavilion with a roof made of national flags. Business people brown bag it on benches at lunchtime as kids cavort in the fountain. You can change your kids out of their wet swimsuits in the small but clean restrooms in the visitor's center, or next door in CNN Center.

What's the next best thing to a voluntary soaking? Watching an unsuspecting tourist posing for a picture in front of the fountain get doused by a surprise burst of water. Kids break into hysterical laughter and, sometimes, even the dampened tourist giggles.

EATS FOR KIDS There are acres of lawn (enough to cover nearby Turner Field three times) just perfect for spreading out a picnic lunch. You can also sit at one of the park's many benches or even on the wall bordering the Fountain of Rings. Right alongside the fountain is the aptly-named **Fountain Side Café** (tel. 404/223–4500), a small eatery that sells hot dogs, pizza, sandwiches, fruit, and cookies. Perch at the counter facing the fountain or choose an umbrella-topped table. CNN Center next door has more than a dozen fast-food options as well as **Jocks & Jills** and **Rimini** (*see* CNN Studio Tour).

I f your kid thinks *Sesame Street* is the coolest, he'll be blown away by the Center for Puppetry Arts, the country's largest organization devoted strictly to the art of puppetry. Tucked away in an old Midtown school building, the center presents a wide array of puppetry performances ranging from well-known classics (Alice in Wonderland, The Velveteen Rabbit) to educational originals (Weather Rocks!, Rainforest Adventures).

The types of puppets used vary from performance to performance. But after each show in the center's two theaters the puppeteers come to the front of the stage and explain how each of the puppets in that production works. From rod to shadow puppets, marionettes to body puppets, you'll get a captivating explanation of the magic behind the movement.

The daytime Family Series shows are less than an hour, so even if your kids are on the fidgety side, it's tough to get bored with the fast pacing and the music numbers. For teens, consider the evening and Sunday afternoon New Directions Series which includes dramas

HEY, KIDS! Create-A-Puppet workshops are offered before and after nearly every show. You'll head to a classroom above the theater (don't worry, there's no homework involved) and get to make a puppet that relates to the show you just saw. There are huge tubs of sequins and buttons and feathers and lots of messy glue involved. There's even a stage in the room so you can put on your own puppet show with your nifty new creation! The workshop lasts 45 minutes.

 1404 Spring St. at 18th St., Midtown

 $10 ages 2 and up; includes admission to museum, special exhibits, and workshop

 Year-round Sa 10, 12, 2 and Su 12, 2; Sept–May, T–F 10 & 11:30; Jun–Aug, T–F 10 & 12. Call for schedules.

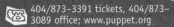 404/873-3391 tickets, 404/873-3089 office; www.puppet.org

3 and up

such as *Live Faust, Die Young* (about a deal with the devil) and *The Baroque Opera* (based on a Czech folk opera).

Get to the center early so you can visit the fascinating museum (T–Sa 9–5, Su 11–5). The interactive "Puppets: The Power of Wonder" includes hundreds of puppets from around the world. Kids can get behind the controls of a baby bird or a giant mythological creature while parents can swoon over original Muppets. There are little doors to open (with puppets inside) and booths for making shadow puppets with your hands.

To savor everything, visit "String Fling," the annual fall weekend fundraiser with performances, puppet-making, backstage tours, and street performers. Year-round behind-the-scene tours ($5) give you a puppeteer's view of backstage and all sorts of curious gadgets.

EATS FOR KIDS
There's nothing to eat at the center but you're welcome to picnic on the lawn. You can get sandwiches and pizza at nearby **Carolyn's Gourmet Café** (1151 W. Peachtree St., tel. 404/607-8100) or famous burgers and fries at **The Varsity** (61 North Ave., tel. 404/881-1706).

KEEP IN MIND A word of caution: there's a loud mechanical phoenix that emerges from a trash can at the museum's entrance that can be quite frightening for the littlest ones. The creature comes alive (complete with loud noises and dramatic lights) when the door shuts behind you. If you think your tyke might be scared ask a staff member to let you go in the back way, or as soon as you enter the museum, quickly open the adjoining door to the next exhibit. Then you can watch from the window where it's not quite so scary.

CHATEAU ÉLAN WINERY & RESORT

There's no moat, but Chateau Élan is about as close as you'll get to a castle this close to Atlanta. Flags flap high atop its two towering roofs, six arched porticos mark the elegant entrance, and a balcony runs nearly the length of the building, which is modeled after a 16th-century French chateau. This upscale resort welcomes even commoners to experience the good life for a day. Your daughter can waltz through the front doors feeling like Cinderella, your son, like Little Lord Fauntleroy.

At the heart of the resort are 200 acres of vineyards and a winery that produces award-winning wines. You're free to meander among the grapevines that are strung out in perfectly straight rows in front of and behind the chateau. Inside, a 10-minute video explains the winemaking process from the planting of the grapes to the importance of timing the harvest just right. The footage shows the mechanized bottling process as rows of green bottles zip along a conveyor to be filled, corked, labeled, and sent packing.

HEY, KIDS!

Way back before they had fancy grape-pressing machines, winemakers physically stomped barefoot on their grapes to make wine! Wanna try it? Every September, Chateau Élan puts on a one-day Vineyard Fest complete with a grape-stomping contest that even kids can join! The most juice wins.

EATS FOR KIDS

There are eight restaurants throughout the Chateau Élan resort, most serving fancy food even at lunchtime. Fortunately, eager-to-please chefs will whip up a standard grilled cheese sandwich or hot dog, if asked. Best bets are **Paddy's Irish Pub** (tel. 678/425–0900, ext. 6074) adjacent to the winery and **Clubhouse Grille** (tel. 678/425–0900, ext. 6075) at the Chateau and Woodland golf courses. You're also welcome to picnic almost anywhere on the grounds (except in the middle of the vineyards). If you forgot to pack some food, there's a castle-like Publix right across the road.

 100 Rue Charlemagne, Braselton

Free

 M–Sa tours begin at 11; Su tours begin at 12

678/425–0900; 770/307–3786
events hotline; www.chateauelan.com

10 and up

The winery tour covers three areas—the chilly vat room filled with shiny fermentation tanks and 60-gallon wooden barrels stacked two stories high, a cask room that allows a peek at the idle bottling assembly line, and a tasting room which is off-limits to guests under 21. Even though there's no grape stomping or smushing going on—and the permeating odor is like grape juice left too long in the fridge—it's impressive to see the two 1,840-gallon casks that are taller than your average elephant. It's not a dungeon, but it will do.

If there's a horse-lover in your house, consider visiting when there's a show at the resort's slick equestrian center. One of the most popular horse show venues in Georgia, it's the site for everything from show-jumping and dressage events to rodeos and pony club shows. Horses trot through the huge covered arena and neighboring four show rings nearly every weekend. All the shows are free to watch and it's a chance for Cinderella to imagine the life of National Velvet.

KEEP IN MIND You won't see the actual winemaking and bottling process unless you visit during harvest time. To catch the mechanical assembly line at work, plan your trip for late summer or early fall when the grapes are being pressed, or when the wine is ready to be bottled. All the activity usually happens in August or September, so call before you visit to make sure you'll see more than empty rooms during your trip.

CHATTAHOOCHEE NATURE CENTER

44

Out in the midst of suburbia, this wildlife refuge follows the bends of the Chattahoochee River. Green frogs float semi-submerged in the beaver pond while Canada geese honk and strut on the grass. Along with the butterflies flitting about and the garden upon garden of native plants, they all call the 127-acre refuge home. The beavers aren't always busy, but they sure draw a crowd. Two beaver siblings lay side-by-side on their backs as if waiting for their brown furry bellies to be scratched. They stretch out their odd, prehistoric-looking webbed feet and occasionally move their big flat tails to the delight of preschoolers hovering on the other side of the fence.

The center's most regal inhabitants are a pair of bald eagles. Perched on a limb only a couple of feet away from the netting that defines his aviary, one handsome bird appears to scowl at visitors. Among the feathered inhabitants of the raptor aviaries, a barn owl and great horned owls swivel their heads all the way around to follow your moves. Red-tailed hawks and black vultures hop from limb to limb as if trying to get a closer look.

HEY, KIDS! When you're in the Discovery Center, look for the aquarium filled with Eastern mud turtles. Can you see them? Probably not! The four-inch turtles spend most of their time burrowing deep in the mud. Because their shells are mostly dark brown, they blend in and are almost impossible to spot. By comparison, it's easy to find the gopher tortoises, which have burrows outside near the beavers. There's a clear window that looks into their burrows so you can see them even when they go underground.

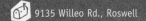
9135 Willeo Rd., Roswell

770/992-2055; www.chattnaturecenter.com

$3 ages 13 and up, $1 children 3–12

M–Sa 9–5, Su 12–5

All ages

Other animal inhabitants such as turtles and snakes reside in the Discovery Center where you can sort through the "touch table" of natural objects such as turtle shells, fossils, animal skulls, feathers, and bones. After years of being handled, some have seen much better days. In the sandbox, kids get absorbed in using the real feet of a porcupine, beaver, fox or snapping turtle to make prints in the sand.

There are walking trails (most are very stroller-friendly) throughout the center, but the most interesting is the half-mile River Boardwalk trail across Willeo Road. Following the Chattahoochee, you'll get up-close looks at the natural habitat of frogs, ducks, muskrats, and swaying cattails. Supposedly, more beavers call this part of the park home but they're not easily found. They must be sleeping.

KEEP IN MIND
If you bring nothing else with you to the Chattahoochee Nature Center, load up on bug spray! So many of the natural habitats are marshy areas—like most of the River Boardwalk trail and the frog pond—where mosquitoes love to hang out.

EATS FOR KIDS For lighter-than-air biscuits and tasty, cheap Southern fare check out the **Southern Skillet** (1037 Alpharetta St., tel. 770/993–7700). Various vegetables, meats, and desserts of the day are posted on big blackboards among the license plates and feed store signs decorating the walls. There's quick pizza and calzones only minutes away at **Johnny's Pizza** (4880 Lower Roswell Road, tel. 678/560–2228). If you'd rather not return to civilization for your lunch, benches on the boardwalk trail provide incredible river views, and some benches overlook the frog pond. Snacks and drinks are sold in the **Nature Store**.

CHILDREN'S ARTS MUSEUM

An 8-foot harp stands sentry in the beautiful glass-enclosed atrium of the Children's Arts Museum just itching to be played. Little fingers grab for the long silver strings and loud yet extremely melodic music reverberates throughout the room. This is obviously no hushed and reverent art museum. It's a forum where kids can dabble in the performing arts as well as view the works of professional artists—and of their peers.

Once inside the actual museum, kids come face to knee with a towering lime-green giraffe sporting a pink mane and a pith helmet. (It's Styrofoam, so kids constantly show off their strength by picking it up.) Welcome to Art Safari, the center's permanent hands-on exhibit. In one kiosk, your aspiring ballerina can wiggle into a pink, blue, or bright purple sequined tutu, twirling on her toes in front of kid-sized mirrors. A powder-blue elephant wearing a yellow tutu and with daisies trimming her tail poses nearby for inspiration.

If your little one is more likely to become the next Tito Puente, skip to the next kiosk

HEY, KIDS!
Poke your head into the museum's gift shop before you leave. Not only is it filled with neat puppets, crafts, and books, it's also home to the back end of a real Gwinnett County school bus sticking out of the wall!

KEEP IN MIND The hustle and bustle of performances, art projects, and storytelling are typical on Saturday, the day when the museum is often overflowing with young artists, thespians, and musicians. On other days of the week you can leisurely explore the interactive kiosks without having to wait in long lines for the well-worn dress-up clothes or at the puppet stage. There are no face painters on hand but you can check out some paint at the front desk to decorate on your own, and there are usually do-it-yourself art projects to tackle, with easy step-by-step instructions.

6400 Sugarloaf Pkwy., Duluth

 $5 ages 3 and up

 Tu–F 1–5, Sa 10–3

770/623–6002;
www.hudgenscenter.org

2 to 10

where pint-sized musicians pass drums and dulcimers back and forth, creating a cacophony of rhythms while dancing about. Kids less inclined to join a crowd can have their face painted, pound on red clay, or draw self-portraits, inspired by tacked-up images by van Gogh and Frida Kahlo.

Adjoining the Art Safari room are rotating exhibits, usually by illustrators of children's books. The colorful artwork is appropriately hung at kids' eye-level and is accompanied by the artist's actual books. With book in hand, ask your children if they can find a picture on the wall that matches the one in the storybook in front of them.

Art made by children throughout the metro Atlanta school systems is displayed in the museum's outer hallways. From kindergartners' finger-paints to elaborate photography projects by high-schoolers, the exhibit shows how kids of all ages have made art. While you're there, give the harp a strum for good measure. Doesn't creativity sound good?

EATS FOR KIDS About three miles away is the fun and noisy **Pepperoni's** (2750 Buford Hwy., tel. 770/232–0224), a neighborhood joint that sells pizza, sandwiches, and pasta. Be sure to get one of the glass-topped tables filled with knick-knacks and toys. There's also the cowboy hangout **Roadhouse Grill** (2000 Satellite Blvd., tel. 770/476–0420), where kids are encouraged to throw their peanut shells on the floor. For messy but inexpensive tacos, fajitas, and burritos, head to **Frontera Mex-Mex Grill** (6555 Sugarloaf Pkwy., tel. 678/474–0831), which also has a patio.

CLAYTON COUNTY BEACH

While metro Atlanta's other water parks are sprawling complexes filled with lots of thrilling slides and have monstrous admission fees to match, The Beach at Clayton County International Park is a smaller, simpler attraction with fewer frills but a much more affordable entrance fee. Home to the beach volleyball matches in the 1996 summer Olympics, the focal point of the water park today is a six-acre manmade lake circled by yards of sandy beach. Tots can sit in the shallow water at the shore while older kids can swim past the roped-off area out to where the water is 10 feet deep. Why swim out so far? To get to the 20-foot-long trampoline in the middle of the lake and do somersaults and back flips before jumping off into the water (a lifeguard attends the trampoline). There are also two basic water slides (minimum height 48") and a geyser-like fountain within the lake.

The water is only 3 feet deep in the smaller kiddie area on the far side of the lake. There, younger kids can romp on little slides, a seesaw, and a smaller trampoline. But the best

KEEP IN MIND Alongside the restrooms at the entrance to the park are large changing areas. There are no showers, but there are plenty of private dressing rooms, benches, and a couple of infant changing tables. If you don't want to take your valuables outside with you and you don't want to leave them in the car, take advantage of the park's free lockers inside the changing areas. Just remember to bring your own lock.

2300 Hwy. 138, Jonesboro

$8 ages 13 and up;
$6 ages 3 to 12

Memorial Day weekend–Labor Day 10–6

770/477–3766;
www.thebeachccip.com

2 and up

little-children's area is the kiddie pool right inside the entrance for kids under 48" tall. Your little guys can board a pirate ship outfitted with different slides, duck under mushroom umbrellas pouring water, and aim at each other with squirting water cannons. There are all sorts of whimsical slides—butterflies, clams, trees—as well as spouting turtles.

You can bring your own chairs to sit on the beach, but if you'd rather not lug them with you, lounge chairs are $3 to rent. Single and double inner tubes for the lake are $2–$3. If your kids like playing in the sand, don't forget your buckets and shovels. The sand on this beach is damp, perfect for packing and making sandcastles.

HEY KIDS! If you're unsure about jumping on that huge trampoline in the middle of the lake by yourself, take a buddy with you. Two people can use the trampoline at the same time. Just jump off when the lifeguard tells you your two minutes are up.

EATS FOR KIDS As long as you leave glass bottles and alcohol at home, you're welcome to pack almost any food and drink into your cooler and take it to the park with you. There are about two dozen picnic tables surrounding the kiddie pool, all under huge umbrellas. A concession stand sells stuffed crust pizza, nachos, cheeseburgers, and hot dogs, as well as a good array of snacks ranging from popcorn and chips to all kinds of candy.

CNN STUDIO TOUR

41

CNN's behind-the-scenes studio tour starts off exciting enough. An eight-story escalator—one of the tallest in the world—transports you high above bustling CNN Center. The escalator, you find out, is built in the area where a roller coaster once stood when the building housed an indoor amusement park. Although you literally go downhill from there (to the studio floors below), the thrills keep coming.

While adults might be intrigued by the news-related artifacts displayed (Larry King's suspenders and a piece of a Gulf War cruise missile), kids tune in when they get to the model control room where they can watch dozens of live feeds and the competitors' broadcasts, as well as live programming. Seeing an off-air, perfectly put-together anchor blow her nose earns plenty of giggles. You might get plucked from the crowd to try your hand at broadcast news. Read the scrolling words of the TelePrompTer (which are

HEY, KIDS!
Pay attention during the control room part of the tour, and you'll see why TV weather people deliver their forecasts while standing sideways. Because there's no actual weather map behind them, they watch themselves on off-camera monitors so they can see where they are pointing.

EATS FOR KIDS Where an ice rink once stood, the CNN Center's first-floor food court is filled with fast-food fare as well as restaurants such as **Jocks & Jills** (tel. 404/688–4225), a sports-theme hangout with more than 90 televisions all over the room and lots of athletic memorabilia on the wall. The menu is typical sports-bar fare with sandwiches and an impressive collection of burgers. In the food court, **Rimini** (tel. 404/584–8955) has pizza-by-the-slice, subs, and spaghetti. Finish off your meal with ice cream or yogurt at **Gorin's** (tel. 404/521–0588). There are plenty of tables indoors, and you can also take your food next door to Centennial Olympic Park.

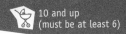
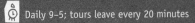
passing right over the camera lens) and voilá, you're ready for live TV. It's even more fun when the tour guide demonstrates how the TV weather map works. He stands in front of a blue screen and, by the wizardry of something called Chroma Key, a map of the U.S. magically appears in the background. When he holds a blue piece of cardboard in front of his face, he appears headless on the monitor. That's pretty cool.

The weather demonstration is more interesting than watching the news go on air. For that part, you stand on a glassed-in balcony overlooking the newsroom, which is basically just a lot of people sitting at a lot of computers. You get to see the back of the anchor's head (and, if you're lucky, more nose blowing!). The kids seem to get a big kick out of finding the producer stuffing his face with a bagel, or the cameraman scratching an itch on the seat of his pants!

KEEP IN MIND If your children are at least 12 years old, they can join you as part of the audience for CNN's *Talkback Live* news show. The show is held in the CNN Center atrium right next to where you line up for the studio tour. Tickets are free but the audience is small so make reservations (tel. 800/410–4CNN). Otherwise, it's first-come, first-served. You never know what the subject will be, and keep in mind that sometimes the topic may be too adult for some children.

CRISSON GOLD MINE

40

You won't strike it rich at the Crisson Gold Mine, but your kids will have a blast. They'll play with water, sand, and rocks, then go home with a prize! Dahlonega, in north Georgia, is rich with gold-mining history. It's the site of the first major gold rush in North America. There are a number of places where you can dig in and pan for gold and gemstones, but one of the most kid-friendly is Crisson, a fourth-generation mine dating back to 1847.

The best start for kids up to about 10 years old is screening for gemstones. It offers instant gratification and big rocks! Kids shovel scoops of sand into a square mesh screen, then dip it in and out of a water trough, watching the sand filter out and the stones remain behind. They shriek with delight as they find amethysts, rubies, sapphires and—every kid's favorite—fool's gold, actually pyrite, a mesmerizing, sparkly gold and silver stone.

Although the gemstones make for bigger results, gold panning is fun for older children. It requires much more patience and skill as kids take a black pan of sand and carefully dip it

KEEP IN MIND It might be a good idea to bring a change of clothes for the kids when you head out to the gold mine. Panning is messy business as would-be prospectors go splashing around elbow deep in the troughs, which are filled with plenty of sandy, murky water. It's a near guarantee that kids will get dirty, or at least very wet! During winter, the mine has covered and heated panning areas when the weather gets cold. Put the kids in short-sleeved shirts (or their sleeves will get soaked!)

in the water, removing a thin layer of sand each time. When done correctly, a few very tiny flecks of gold remain in the bottom of the pan. You can pop the precious finds into small keepsake vials. If the panning seems fruitless, a mine employee will gladly pitch in and help find treasure. (They never let anyone go home empty-handed.)

You'll be stooped over the troughs concentrating on your finds until you hear a loud grinding sound as the 1883 stamp mill kicks into gear. Join the panners hurrying up the hillside to see the machine at work. The massive piece of equipment grinds rocks into sand, which is then washed down the hill into the panning area below. The 20-foot contraption is incredibly loud, but when you watch it work, you realize there really is gold in them thar hills.

HEY, KIDS! Have you ever seen the gold-covered dome of the Georgia State Capitol building in downtown Atlanta? Nearly one-third of the gold covering that dome came from the Crisson Mine in Dahlonega. Of the Capitol's 52 ounces of gold, 16 ounces were mined right here.

EATS FOR KIDS Just 2 1/2 miles down the road, **Zaxby's** (58 Pine Tree Way, tel. 706/867–0937) specializes in chicken and has chicken fingers and grilled cheese for kids. There are all sorts of nice little neighborhood restaurants in downtown Dahlonega, less than two miles away. On the square, **Jack's Café** (44 Public Square South, tel. 706/864–4664) has lots of basic sandwiches. Take a look at the square's action from above at **The Front Porch** (72 Public Square North, tel. 706/864–0124), which serves hot dogs, sandwiches, and ice cream.

DUNWOODY NATURE CENTER

A mid all the pristine neighborhoods, landscaped yards, and quaint little shops in Dunwoody, there's a big chunk of wilderness ripe for exploring. This 22-acre preserve is a no-frills nature center that offers lots of programs for children, plus two miles of trails that wind up and down hills, across a creek, and through a meadow.

In the center's main building, poke through the small compost exhibit to find the worms who live there. Kids shriek happily when one of the little squiggly brown creatures is uncovered in the mix of newspaper strips and fruit. You can pick your way over and around art projects and nature exhibits, look for the critter camouflaged in the terrarium (it's a Daddy Long-legs), and measure yourself in the hallway against the wingspans of hawks and owls. A constant buzz draws kids to the glassed-in observation beehive. The workers zip in and out through a tube that leads to the pollinators' paradise garden where alongside the

HEY, KIDS!

Did you notice the branch lying in the garden's small pond? It's there so frogs will have a place to rest and, if a squirrel or chipmunk happens to splash in, he'll have something to grab hold of so he can get out.

EATS FOR KIDS Plenty of dining options await less than a half mile down the road, in downtown Dunwoody. **My Friend's Place** (5533 Chamblee Dunwoody Rd., tel. 770/396–1128) has grilled cheese, peanut butter and jelly, and an array of mini-sand-wiches. (They'll even offer to cut the crust off.) Huge cookies and cake slices are on the dessert menu. For more ethnic cuisine, there's tacos and burritos at **Mexico City Gourmet** (5500 Chamblee Dunwoody Rd., tel. 770/396–1111) which is festively hung with strands of colored lights. For pizza, there's the funkily decorated **Mel-low Mushroom** (5575 Chamblee Dunwoody Rd., tel. 770/396–1393).

 5343 Roberts Dr., Dunwoody

770/394-3322; www.
dunwoodynature.org

 Free

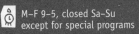 M–F 9–5, closed Sa–Su
except for special programs

 2 and up

honeybees, butterflies dance about the milkweed and marigolds. "Don't bother them and they won't bother you," a hand-lettered sign suggests.

While the birds trill and the resident honeybees swarm to and from their indoor hive, there's an awful lot of splashing and laughter down by Wildcat Creek. A dozen summer campers wade through the water, scooping up water striders and crawdads in plastic cups. They call out for the huge 50-year old turtle that lives on the shore, but she's hiding somewhere among the jewel weed. Bright blue damselflies flit about near the babbling creek as a couple of children chase them, hoping one will land on their hands so they can have a closer look. In case your preschooler prefers man-made distraction, there's a mini-playground to the side of one trail with a tire swing and a couple of tree houses. Most kids seem perfectly satisfied tromping through the woods, though.

KEEP IN MIND The center is well known for its programs and activities, including a very active summer camp and two-hour monthly hikes (Saturdays, May–Sept, $10/members $12/non-members, per family) led by guides who identify the flora and fauna. Throughout the school year, the Curiosity Clubs offer kids 2 and up all sorts of nature encounters. Morning classes for toddlers are essentially storytelling times with environmental themes. Preschoolers and older children play scientists and naturalists in once-a-week after-school programs (fees and times vary).

ESPN X-GAMES SKATEPARK

If you have a pre-teen or teenage son who does death-defying antics on his skateboard or skates, have him perfect the death-defying part at this indoor park. The two-hour sessions for inline skating, skateboarding, and BMX bike-riding are open to ages 6 and up. Skateboarders and inline skaters pull stunts together but riders have separate sessions, usually in the evenings. While yours is polishing his moves, you can keep a close eye on him...or go shopping. Attached to the park is the sprawling Discover Mills mall.

The 40,000 square feet of ramps, ledges, and half-pipes is surrounded by a handful of padded poles and patrolled by first aid–certified attendants. If your kids are just learning, there's a beginner area with small ramps for practicing simple maneuvers. If they know what they're doing, they'll probably head for some of the scarier ramps (some as high as 12 feet). You can watch from the elevated observation deck or from a table at the edge of the course.

EATS FOR KIDS Besides the usual options lined up on both sides of the food court, there's **Jillian's** (tel. 678/847–5400) at the same end of the mall as the skatepark. Half entertainment complex, half restaurant, Jillian's has bowling and virtual bowling along with the chili, burgers, and pizza. For pitas, nachos, and tacos, check out **Chili's Too** (tel. 678/847–5910) in the middle of the mall. Near the food court is **Johnny Rockets** (tel. 678/847–5800) where you'll find egg salad, chili dogs, and BLT's in addition to their signature all-American burgers, shakes, and fries.

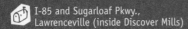 I-85 and Sugarloaf Pkwy.,
Lawrenceville (inside Discover Mills)

 678/847-5727; http://expn.go.
com/skt/s/parkprev.html

 2-hour session $11–14
for non-members,
$7–9 for members; $45
for membership

 10AM–11PM daily

 10 and up

To keep younger children entertained while the daredevils do their thing, there's fun at the opposite end of the mall. Huge fish and a sunken rowboat fill the 50-foot-long aquarium at **Bass Pro Shops Outdoor World** (tel. 678/847-5500). Kids can sit on the trout-shaped benches and spot bigmouth buffaloes or channel catfish with the help of the identification chart that's posted. There's also an indoor waterfall on the other side of a climbing wall ($3/climb; must weigh at least 50 pounds) and you can hunt for real (mounted) animals like moose and grizzly bears throughout the store.

Also in the mall near the skatepark are exhibit cases from the **Georgia Music and Sports Hall of Fame**. Young Bucky Lasek and Fabiola da Silva might not have their wheels here yet, but check out country singer Alan Jackson's jeans and hightops, as well as uniforms from the Braves, Thrashers, and Falcons.

KEEP IN MIND
All skaters and riders must have a signed liability waiver. Parents or guardians of kids under 18 must sign the form in the presence of a skatepark employee. If you can't go with your child, you must sign and notarize a form before sending her or him off with it.

HEY KIDS! Safety is important whenever you're racing around on a set of wheels. You're not allowed to enter the skating area of the park unless you're wearing at least a helmet, knee pads, and elbow pads. Inline skaters should also wear wrist guards. You should already have all that safety equipment but if you forget it, you can rent a helmet and pads ($5 per session) at the park. It may be tempting to try somersaults off the 7- and 10-foot ramps into the foam pit. Don't! It's too dangerous, and you'll be asked to leave the park.

FERNBANK MUSEUM OF NATURAL HISTORY

37

Forget Barney. Towering in Fernbank's Great Hall are replicas of the world's largest dinosaurs—long-necked Argentinosaurus and his nasty nemesis, Gigantosaurus. About the length of three school buses, Argentinosaurus is the only specimen of his kind on display in the world. Kids can peer at the creatures from all three levels of the museum.

Although the dinosaurs are a crowd-pleaser, the real hands-on action for kids is in Sensing Nature, a gallery that lets future scientists do everything from create humongous bubbles to watch tornadoes form to deliver the forecast on The Weather Channel. Curious kids (to inquisitive adults) can tinker with shadows, lights, and magnets to investigate all sorts of natural phenomena. Just try to touch the disappearing metal spring or figure out how you can be heard all the way across the room even if you whisper.

There are still more dinosaurs in the midst of "A Walk Through Time in Georgia," an 18-gallery exhibit that follows the state's geographic regions throughout history. Highlights

EATS FOR KIDS The museum's lower level dining room offers all sorts of reasonably priced snacks and meals including pizza, hot dogs, and sandwiches. You're also welcome to picnic on the vast front lawn or the back terrace, which overlooks the edge of Fernbank Forest.

HEY KIDS! Be sure to stop by the nature discovery cart parked on the lower level of the museum right at the biggest dinosaurs' feet. A volunteer will let you touch some cool fossils and fossil replicas—including an enormous dinosaur tooth! Ask for some tracing paper and a pencil, and you can scout the museum's fossil-filled limestone tile floor for the actual remains of marine creatures such as sponges and ammonites that were alive more than 150 million years ago! Trace them for your own souvenirs.

  767 Clifton Rd., N.E., Druid Hills

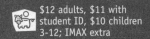 $12 adults, $11 with student ID, $10 children 3-12; IMAX extra

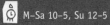 M–Sa 10–5, Su 12–5

404/929–6300; www.fernbank.edu/museum

 3 and up

include a hatching baby hadrosaur and an icky, slime-covered giant ground sloth. Patient kids might enjoy the Okefenokee Swamp re-creation where if they wait four minutes, they can see day to turn to night. (Croaking frogs and hooting owls replace songbirds and sunshine.)

There are two discovery rooms for children on the top floor. Fantasy Forest is most appealing to the youngest preschoolers who are amused by feeding stuffed worms to pretend baby birds and watching flowers blossom as they "pollinate" them with balls. The Georgia Adventure is aimed at 6–9 year olds but it's the younger kids who will most enjoy fishing off a rowboat, climbing a mountain, and building a city.

The museum is also home to an IMAX cinema that features films about scenic, far-off lands and risk-taking adventurers. Young children might be overwhelmed by the gigantic (five stories/72-feet-high) screen and overpowering sound.

KEEP IN MIND The museum's bubble pros offer some handy tips if you want to try it at home. Mix up a soapy solution and let it sit for at least five days. (The aging dramatically improves the solution's bubble-making ability.) If you're hunting for the absolute best bubbles, Fernbank researchers suggest Dawn dishwashing liquid.

FERNBANK SCIENCE CENTER

Not quite as slick as its counterpart, the Fernbank Museum of Natural History, the Fernbank Science Center is still an entertaining educational destination—especially for wannabe astronauts or astronomers.

The circular, bi-level exhibit hall has an eclectic array of science- and nature-themed displays. The space-obsessed can marvel at the command module of Apollo 6 and a real spacesuit from an Apollo mission. There are busts of famous astronauts and meteorites as big as soccer balls, plus AEL, a NASA-funded aeronautics lab for students and summer day campers.

Down-to-earth exhibits include lots of stuffed animals (of the taxidermy, not the teddy-bear type) that grab the attention of even the littlest kids. A snarling saber-toothed tiger shows off some impressive dagger-like teeth. There's an entire case filled with once-slithering snakes and huge displays of colorful birds, bears, and rodents.

EATS FOR KIDS There's no food at the science center but you can brown bag it on the lawn. For sit-down fare check out the funky decor and good pizzas at nearby **Fellini's** (923 Ponce de Leon Ave., tel. 404/873–3088) or the Z-burgers and mile-high ice cream cones at **Zesto** (544 Ponce de Leon Ave., tel. 404/607–1118). Fifteen minutes away is the world's largest drive-in, the famous **Varsity** (61 North Ave., tel. 404/881–1706), where burgers, chilidogs, and frosted oranges score the most points. Kids can clown around in the commemorative paper hats.

 156 Heaton Park Dr., N.E., Druid Hills

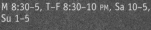 Free; family planetarium shows $2 all ages

404/378-4311; http://fsc.fernbank.edu

 M 8:30–5, T–F 8:30–10 PM, Sa 10–5, Su 1–5

3 and up

Fernbank's planetarium includes shows geared specifically toward families on Saturday and Sunday at 1:30. The programs are only 30 minutes long (instead of the usual 45) and are open to kids of all ages. Kids are asked to look for constellations and answer questions about what they see. In summer, family planetarium shows are also held at 11 and 1:30 Tuesday through Friday.

For a look at the real night sky, bring your kids to Fernbank's observatory. You can peer through the largest telescope in the southeastern U.S. as well as a number of smaller telescopes stationed throughout the observatory deck. The observatory is open to the public on Thursday and Friday nights starting at nightfall, weather permitting. It'll give "Twinkle, Twinkle Little Star" a whole new meaning.

KEEP IN MIND
Young children are discouraged from attending Fernbank's standard planetarium shows. Though educational, these programs are darker, louder, and longer than family shows. However, older kids and teens are welcome. Program times vary but are usually held Wednesday through Friday at 8 PM, with 3:30 weekend matinees.

HEY KIDS! Stare up at the planetarium ceiling once it's filled with stars, and try to count them all. You'll be counting all night! There are somewhere around 8,900 stars up there as well as the sun, moon, and planets. They come from that enormous planetarium projector in the middle of the room. It's made up of 200 different projectors that shoot images onto the ceiling to make the picture of the night sky. There are 250 more projectors throughout the room that provide special effects and videos.

FUNKY CHICKEN ART PROJECT

A steep gravel road leads to the funkiest poultry barn you could ever imagine. A life-size mermaid sculpture with strands of copper-wire hair hovers at the entrance surrounded by glass-and-bead wind chimes, huge flower sculptures, and stone-encrusted concrete planters shaped like the heads of sheep. Four-, five-, and six-foot high metal suns, moons, dragonflies, and sunflowers rise up all over the yard. Kids are beside themselves staring at all the far-out stuff, and they haven't even been through the door yet.

The Funky Chicken is a former chicken house that the artist owners converted into an art gallery. They keep real chickens in backyard coops—strictly for ambience (not eating) purposes. Like the outdoor art, the indoor work is all contemporary and fun. Two-foot high chicken statues wearing sneakers and holding pinwheels compete for kids' attention with a clay angel who has old New York license plates for wings. On the weekend local artists sell their work and often do demonstrations in the building behind the main gallery.

HEY, KIDS!

Look for the work of artist Scott Cousino. Through his other job as a welder he finds odd metal pieces that he turns into sculptures like bugs made of pistons and gears. It's tempting to touch, but be respectful of all the art by just looking. (Is that why they call it "visual art?")

KEEP IN MIND Although nearly all the art at the Funky Chicken is whimsical, fun, and attention-grabbing, it might not be the best place for those who don't understand the phrase "don't touch!" The art is very enticing so be sure your kids are able to resist the temptation to touch before letting them loose. Or else you may go home with a lot of (broken) artwork! The gallery and garden are not stroller-friendly so take kids by the hand as they wander around.

 1538 Wesley Chapel Rd., Dahlonega

 Free

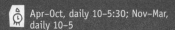 Apr–Oct, daily 10–5:30; Nov–Mar, daily 10–5

 706/864-3938; www.funkychickenartproject.com

5 and up

Out back, you can meander through the paths of the sculpture garden, taking in the huge purple bird made out of salvaged parts like rebar and rusty bolts. But the creation that draws the most curiosity is a metal alien with a butterfly on his odd little finger.

The dozen coops house all sorts of colorful creatures like brilliantly colored golden seabrights and large strutting Saipan jungle fowl. Chickens, pheasants, and a peacock chatter in the background while at least one noisy rooster crows loudly for attention. Depending on when you visit, there's often the chance that newly hatched chicks will be scurrying about, or maybe there will even be recently laid eggs in the straw. On your way out, let the kids say good-bye to Guida, the blue and gold macaw who squawks her greetings at the front door.

EATS FOR KIDS The closest place to eat is four miles away at the **Maple Restaurant** (Hwy. 52, tel. 706/265–8888; *see* Amicalola Falls State Park). Other than that, you'll have to drive at least 20 minutes. In Dawsonville across from the Courthouse, there's the **Finish Line Restaurant** (11 Hwy. 9, tel. 706/265–1859) packed with an array of deli sandwiches, plus grilled cheese and hot dogs. In Dahlonega, try **Jack's Café** (44 Public Square South, tel. 706/864–9169) for sandwiches or **Caruso's** (19B E. Main St., tel. 706/864–4664) for pizza.

THE GARDENS AT CALLAWAY

There is far more than rosebushes at Callaway. Your kids can have encounters with butterflies and eagles, vegetables, and acrobats throughout the 14,000-acre gardens.

Hummingbirds and some 1,000 butterflies live among lush foliage and a sparkling waterfall in the glass-enclosed Cecil B. Day Butterfly Center. If you sit quietly on a bench, chances are a butterfly will eventually land on you. Stop by the glass case at the center's entrance and you might be lucky enough to see a butterfly emerge from a chrysalis hanging inside.

From Memorial Day to Labor Day, surf's up at the mile-long Robin Lake Beach, reportedly the largest inland man-made white sand beach in the world. There's a playground, putt-putt golf, paddleboats, and a small, working train. The adjoining Beach Dome becomes a big top every June through mid-August as Florida State University's "Flying High" Circus takes up residence for free shows (performances every day but Wednesday).

KEEP IN MIND From late November through late December, Callaway puts on its Fantasy in Lights, an outdoor holiday display made up of more than eight million lights. You can visit the Gardens during the day, then drive or take an open-air trolley through the lights at night while making stops in a snack- and craft-filled Christmas Village. ($12 adults, $6 ages 6–12 if you drive; $14 adults, $7 ages 6–12 for the trolley.) Tickets go on sale at the end of October, and if you want to visit on a weekend, Thanksgiving, or during the two weeks before Christmas, make reservations for an exact time as soon as possible.

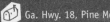 Ga. Hwy. 18, Pine Mountain

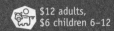 $12 adults,
$6 children 6-12

 Daily 9-5

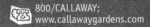 800/CALLAWAY;
www.callawaygardens.com

 All ages

If the only fruits and veggies your kids see are at the supermarket, let them tromp through Mr. Cason's Vegetable Garden. Depending on the season, your kids can see everything from broccoli to kiwi, corn to peas, being tilled, planted, harvested, or watered. (Be sure to let your kids peek into the icky worm bins for a lesson in composting!)

Many of the park's miles of walking trails, like the Wildflower Trail, provide stroller-friendly footing. That trail goes by the Discovery Amphitheater, home to daily Birds of Prey shows (times vary; check the daily events board in the Discovery Center). For the best up-close look at a falcon, owl, and even a bald eagle, grab a front row or aisle seat. The birds soar down the middle aisle at speeds as fast as 200 mph!

HEY, KIDS! If a butterfly lands on you, chances are he's tasting you! Butterflies actually "taste" with their feet, checking to see if the plant they've landed on is the kind they're looking for. Don't worry, you won't be dinner! Most butterflies eat flower nectar and pollen.

EATS FOR KIDS Hundreds of tables for picnicking dot the grounds. You can buy a sandwich or salad and bring it to a table of the lakeside **Discovery Café** (tel. 706/66-2281). Don't feed the ducks that beg for treats because bread isn't good for them! Outside the gates, there's the **Plantation Room** (tel. 706/663-2281) at The Mountain Creek Inn featuring all-day buffets (kids 5 and under eat free). For Southern fare such as chicken and dumplings, fried catfish, and grilled cheese on Texas toast, go a couple miles south to the **Country Kitchen** (U.S. Hwy. 27, tel. 706/663-2281).

GEORGIA INTERNATIONAL HORSE PARK

Girls are in horse heaven here. They hang on the miles of white fence, watching powerful thoroughbreds vault over soaring jumps and canter rhythmically around perfect rings. They can wander the barn aisles, patting the snouts that stick out of stalls, and watching as horses are groomed, fed, and dolled-up with braided manes and tails. Corgis and Dalmatians pad about, saddles squeak, and there's the constant clop-clop of hooves in every direction. It's exciting even for kids who haven't read *Black Beauty*.

Built for the equestrian and mountain-biking events of the 1996 Olympic games, the park is 1,400 acres of fields, rings, barns, and a soon-to-be-built nature preserve. From early March to late November there's a horse show nearly every weekend (which often continues into the week). The rest of the time the events run the gamut from hot air balloon festivals and Frisbee tournaments to concerts and Civil War reenactments. Nearly all the events are free.

KEEP IN MIND Each March, the horse park is home to the Cherry Blossom Festival, a two-day event with lots of food, performances, arts and crafts (like origami and Bonsai tree trimming), pageants, and plenty of shows and activities geared just to children.

EATS FOR KIDS Concession stands around the park sell hot dogs, pretzels, and popcorn. For a real meal, it's best to drive a couple miles into historic downtown Conyers, which is packed with neighborhood shops and restaurants. **Main Street Delicatessen** (896 Main St., tel. 770/929–8300) makes a mean grilled cheese sandwich and homemade hamburgers. Around the corner you can belly-up to the counter of **Evans Pharmacy** (933 Center St., tel. 770/483–7211) and sip a milkshake or root beer float from the old-fashioned soda fountain. It's near **The Sandwich Factory** (903 Commercial St., tel. 770/483–0151), which carries all types of sandwiches.

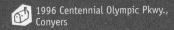
1996 Centennial Olympic Pkwy.,
Conyers

770/860–4190;
www.conyersga.com

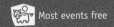 Most events free

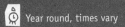 Year round, times vary

 5 and up

When you attend a horse show, find the show office to get a program or ask what's going on where. Events are usually held simultaneously in numerous rings. In hunter/jumper events, the horse and rider have to clear the jumps while making fast time. Dressage is more like equine ballet. Western events can range from showmanship (how a competitor handles her horse) to barrel racing and rodeos.

For an up close look at all things horsey, head over to the vendors who cater to the competitors. You can peek into shiny and cavernous horse trailers, run your hand over gleaming leather bridles and imported saddles, and maybe even try on a velvet-covered riding helmet or a pair of black boots. Most competitors are quite obliging when horse-crazy young spectators ask to pet their horses. If you can't own a horse, at least you can get close to them here.

HEY, KIDS! Across the road from the main horse show area are acres of fields and forests that will become the park's nature preserve. Take a walk over and check out some of the cool jumps that were used in the Olympic horse events. There are huge jumps made out of telephone poles that are shaped like the Olympic rings. There's a wooden covered bridge the horses jumped through and all sorts of steep and scary-looking creations made out of rocks and trees. They're so big you wonder why the horses weren't the ones who won the medals!

GEORGIA STATE CAPITOL

The gold-domed capitol, topped by Miss Freedom, is easily the most distinctive building in downtown Atlanta's skyline. The capitol is home to all the state's major political offices including that of the Governor. If your kids are studying civics or history, this is a good place to get a first-hand look at the state political system.

The tour desk is directly across from the governor's offices, huge rooms with big glass windows that look out on the marble hallway. You might actually see the state's chief executive hustling off to a meeting or to the helipad out front. Tours usually start in the rotunda, surrounded by portraits and busts of some key leaders in Georgian and American history. While most people can pick out George Washington and Ben Franklin, other not-so-recognizable faces include James Edward Oglethorpe (Georgia's founder) and William Few (one of Georgia's signers of the U.S. Constitution). Nearly all the building materials you see inside—the marble on the walls and the iron ore columns—are Georgia products, one of the requirements when the building was constructed in 1889.

EATS FOR KIDS Across the street is **Sylvia's** (241 Central Ave., tel. 404/529–9692), a soul food hangout that has a sister diner in Harlem, New York City. Known for spicy ribs, Southern fried chicken, and sweet potato pie, the restaurant also has a kid's menu with catfish fingers, spaghetti, and pizza. Within easy walking distance is Underground Atlanta, with its bustling food court (*see* World of Coca-Cola). Nearby are all-American milk shakes and burgers at **Johnny Rockets** (50 Upper Alabama St., tel. 404/525–7117), as well as **Mick's** (75 Upper Alabama St., tel. 404/525–2825), offering grilled sandwiches and entrées as well as a vast kid's menu.

214 State Capitol,
Downtown

Free

Tours Jan–Mar (during legislative session),
9:30, 10:30, 1 & 2; April–Dec, 10, 11, 1 & 2

404/656–2844;
www.sos.state.ga.us

8 and up

If you visit when the legislature is in session (typically the second Monday of January through March), you can duck into the balcony of the House of Representatives and the Senate to see the legislative process at work. Your kids might not understand much of what's being said, but it's difficult to miss the importance of the scene. The legislators sit at carved wooden desks, pressing brass buttons to vote, call for a page, ask a question, or ask permission to make a speech.

Just when all the formality and history may get a bit overwhelming, the fourth floor Capitol Museum comes to the rescue. Among the state artifacts behind the glass cases are a mounted two-headed calf and a two-headed snake that once called Georgia home. Unlike the governor, they're always guaranteed to be around for a photo opportunity.

HEY KIDS! There's a lot to see in the Capitol Museum besides the two-headed creatures. Look for a flying squirrel, a 219-pound meteorite that fell to earth in Georgia, a wheel from a Six Flags roller coaster, and Miss Freedom's broken torch that was struck by lightning.

KEEP IN MIND Generally, the least-crowded tour is the first one of the day. Reservations are only necessary for parties of 10 or more. But you don't have to take a guided tour to visit the capitol. The building is open to the public weekdays, 8–5. Just pick up an information booklet at the tour desk inside the main entrance, then wander around on your own. Be sure to walk through the second-floor rotunda, the fourth-floor public galleries of the House and the Senate chambers, and the fourth-floor Capitol Museum.

GONE WITH THE WIND MOVIE MUSEUM

I f you have a teen or "tween" who dreams about "Lights! Camera! Action!" let him explore this museum dedicated to *Gone With the Wind* that also offers a look at Hollywood in the 1930s. The largest private collection of *GWTW* movie memorabilia in the world was amassed by James Tumblin, the retired head of Universal Studios' makeup department. Tumblin insisted the collection's permanent home should be in the South, the book's setting. So it found a home just off Marietta Square.

Not all of the collection's 300,000 pieces are on view but what's here is impressive. There's Vivien Leigh's Oscar, Clark Gable's signed movie contract, Tara's front doorknob, and an original 356-page script. But the memorabilia that wows the most young girls are the dozen costumes that include Scarlett's straw hat from the famous barbecue scene, Belle Watling's shocking red velvet lace-trimmed bodice, and Rhett Butler's black tuxedo. Demonstrating what sticklers the costume designers were for details is an elaborate cotton underskirt that was worn by Vivien Leigh—but not seen by viewers.

KEEP IN MIND Although younger kids will probably get bored at the museum, they'd have a blast playing and climbing on the train at Marietta Square. It even has a bell that rings, and a slide out the back.

EATS FOR KIDS All types of restaurants line Marietta Square. Just down the street from the museum is the **Marietta Pizza Co.** (3 Whitlock Ave., tel. 770/419–0900) serving oven-baked subs, calzones, and pizza by the slice. There's outdoor seating if you want to do some people watching. On the other corner of the square, **Tommy's** (148 Roswell St., tel. 770/422–3185) is a no-frills sandwich shop with everything available in small and large sizes. For dessert, stroll on over to **Sarah Jean's** (109 N. Park Square, tel. 770/424–5177) for old-fashioned hand-dipped ice cream, shakes, floats, and sundaes.

 18 Whitlock Ave.,
off Marietta Square, Marietta

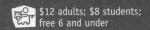 $12 adults; $8 students;
free 6 and under

 M–Sa 10–5, Su 12–5

 770/794–5576;
www.city.marietta.ga.us

 10 and up

There's also the beautiful flouncy blue dress she wore under a coat so only a bit of the sleeves were visible.

The museum also displays some of author Margaret Mitchell's diaries, but the focus here is definitely on the movie, not the book. There are also glimpses of what the whole Hollywood process was like. Check out the intricately painted pictures that served as storyboards for some of the movie's biggest scenes, the original score written in pencil, and incredibly detailed blueprints for stained glass windows that appear only briefly in the film.

A screening room in the back of the museum occasionally runs outtakes and screen tests for the movie as well as other work done by some of the famous cast members. (George Reeves, who played one of the Tarleton twins, went on to become TV's Superman.)

HEY KIDS! When producer David O. Selznick had to clear the studio backlot to build the Tara plantation home, he decided to film the "burning of Atlanta" scene first. By torching old sets from movies like *King Kong* and *The Last of the Mohicans*, he got his fire scene and room to construct Tara. In the museum, check out the "before" and "after" photos of the set. The burning scene was shot before the role of Scarlett had even been cast. While Selznick watched the set burn, his brother Myron introduced him to a young actress named Vivien Leigh. "I'd like you to meet your Scarlett O'Hara," he said.

HASTINGS NATURE & GARDEN CENTER

Even before they step through the doors, kids know this is no ordinary plant store. Next to the entrance a big "Bee Careful" sign points to a private portal that bees use to zoom in and out of Hastings' very own bee hive. Inside the store, kids can safely make their own beeline to the Plexiglas case housing the busy bee colony. In the same area, rabbits, guinea pigs, and a rose-haired tarantula shuffle about their big cages. Could it be any cooler that the creatures are parked next to the free popcorn?

Keep some pennies handy, for you'll surely be asked for some to throw into the wishing well. Most kids aim for the concrete lion that spits out a steady stream of water. Mickey, a scarlet macaw, shouts "Hello! Hello!" immediately drawing a flock of kids to his cage. The geckos are silent but just as magnetic, as kids marvel at the way the lizards suction themselves to the side of their aquarium walls.

KEEP IN MIND Although Hastings is a very kid-friendly place, it's not very stroller-friendly. It's often difficult to steer even the shopping wagons through the crowded aisles, over hoses, and away from sprinklers. Likewise, it's easy to lose track of the kids as they're running over the bridges and around the train and peering into all the ponds. The best spot to park the kids while you shop is the area around the train. There's enough there to keep them interested, and it's partially enclosed so it'll help keep them from wandering off.

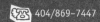 3920 Peachtree Rd., Buckhead

 Free

 M–F 9–7, Sa 8–6, Su 10–6

404/869–7447

All ages

Outside, Spike, a 3-foot-long green iguana lolls lazily in his cage. He's weird-looking, but doesn't do much, so he's forsaken for the chugging model train in the Railroad Garden. Children race around the perimeter following the train as it bypasses a miniature village, ducks through tunnels, and crosses a running stream. The area is surrounded with benches so you can keep an eye on your loved ones (or on the perennials).

For kids with money burning holes in their pockets, there are a slew of children's gardening supplies, books, and toys. For only a couple of dollars, they can go home the proud owner of a tadpole. The frogs-in-training swim around a big black rubber tub, some just beginning to sprout little legs. Of course there's still the turtle pond, the playhouse, the snakes, and the yellow-headed cockatiels. If only the grocery store could be this much fun.

HEY, KIDS! See those huge fish swimming around outside in the five connected ponds? They look like goldfish but they are really koi, a kind of goldfish cousin. Unlike goldfish, these guys can grow up to three feet long. That's about as tall as a 3-year-old kid!

EATS FOR KIDS With its brightly painted walls and inexpensive prices, **Bajarito's** (3877 Peachtree Rd., tel. 404/239–9727), across the street, is a quick kid-friendly spot for Mexican food. Award-winning pizza is a block down at **Mellow Mushroom** (4058 Peachtree Rd., tel. 404/266–1661) where the funky '70s décor on the walls keeps kids entertained. For dessert, head to the walk-up window across the street at **Bruster's Old Fashioned Ice Cream** (3857 Peachtree Rd., tel. 404/231–1195) for a scoop of "cotton candy explosion" or a dinosaur sundae.

HELEN, GEORGIA

There's no doubt about it. Helen is a bit on the kitsch-y side. Tucked into the gorgeous Blue Ridge Mountains in north Georgia, Helen is a re-creation of an old-world alpine village complete with cobblestone streets, peaked Bavarian towers, and lots of gingerbread trim. The town has looked this way since the 1960s, when some local businessmen came up with the German theme as a way to revitalize the town and bring in some tourist dollars. Filled with the usual tourist draws—T-shirt stands, homemade candy shops, and craft stores—Helen also has some attractions for kids who might not appreciate the difference between a hot dog and a good bratwurst.

On the outskirts of downtown Helen at the **Black Forest Bear Park** (8160 S. Main St., tel. 706/878–7043) kids eagerly peer over the sides of huge concrete pits holding the bears in each pen below. Two Asian bears pace in front of their sparkling blue pool. A lounging grizzly lazily opens his mouth, waiting for you to toss in a treat, then lumbers over to lie down in his pool. Two black bear cubs wrestle playfully while a cinnamon bear stands

HEY, KIDS!

Check out the glockenspiel, a traditional German clock, inside the gingerbread house at Charlemagne's Kingdom. Every day at noon, 3, and 6, the glockenspiel plays and six four-foot tall wooden carved German dancers come out marching and dancing in a circle to traditional German music.

EATS FOR KIDS At the **Alt Heidelberg Restaurant** (8660 White Horse Square, tel. 706/873–3273) the kid's menu includes bratwurst, knockwurst, and good old hot dogs and grilled cheese. The Swiss owner walks around wearing lederhosen and carries an orang-utan puppet who "talks." At the jungle-theme **Cannibal's** (8717 N Main St., tel. 706/878–2083) the menu is all-American with hot dogs and chicken nuggets for kids. Halfway between Helen and Cleveland, the **West Family Restaurant** (1963 Tom Bell Rd., Cleveland, tel. 706/865–0525) offers an inexpensive menu and an all-you-can eat family buffet with fried chicken, fresh vegetables, and ice cream.

 85 miles north of downtown Atlanta via GA400 or I-85

 800/858-8027; www.helenga.org

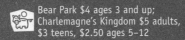 Bear Park $4 ages 3 and up; Charlemagne's Kingdom $5 adults, $3 teens, $2.50 ages 5–12

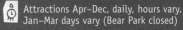 Attractions Apr–Dec, daily, hours vary. Jan–Mar days vary (Bear Park closed)

 3 and up

on her haunches, doing a relatively graceful little dance. A dollar buys you a tray of bear snacks (apples, bread, and the occasional donut). Another dollar gets you into the reptile exhibit—a bunch of snakes—in the back of the gift shop.

At the other end of town Thomas the Tank Engine fans press their noses against the glass at **Charlemagne's Kingdom** (8808 N. Main St., tel. 706/878–2200) where model trains chug around a miniature re-creation of Germany. In the huge 20-foot by 50-foot exhibit hall, hot air balloonists soar across the sky, looking down on 22-foot mountains, a car-packed autobahn, an Oktoberfest with moving carnival rides, and thousands of hand-painted figurines.

There are public parking lots and restrooms throughout downtown. The crowds are thickest in fall when the leaves are changing colors in the surrounding mountains. In summer, it's usually a few degrees cooler here than in Atlanta.

KEEP IN MIND Up in this part of Georgia, the Chattahoochee runs clear and gently. There are a number of rafting companies, such as **Cool River Tubing** (590 Edelweiss Dr., tel. 800/896–4595) and **Flea Market Tubing** (9917 Hwy. 75 N, tel. 706/878–1082) that rent big, colorful inner tubes for trips down the river. Most run between $3–5 per person for an hour's float. The water is fairly smooth. Even toddlers are welcome to climb aboard. The companies will tie the tubes together for a family armada and provide life vests all around.

THE HERNDON HOME

This 1910 mansion is the legacy of one of Atlanta's most prominent African-American families. Born into slavery, Alonzo Herndon became a sharecropper and eventually made his fortune through the Atlanta Life Insurance Company that he founded, as well as through his upscale downtown barbershop. Now a national historic landmark, the home he built is filled with mostly original furnishings and mementos from the Herndon family's life.

Opulence pervades, from the fancy beveled glass windows at the entrance to the intricate parquet floors and the elaborate grandfather clock at the top of the stairs. The home even had the luxury of central heat and electricity as well as indoor plumbing, all of which were rare luxuries in the early 1900s. Be sure your kids see the painted mural on the library's far wall, which represents the stages of Alonzo Herndon's life. The four panels show a Sphinx (denoting the family's African roots), a slave mother and child, a sharecropper working in the field, and a portrait of the Herndon Home. Throughout the

EATS FOR KIDS For a bit of history, take the kids to **Paschal's** (830 Martin Luther King Jr. Dr., tel. 404/577–3150), a Southern-style restaurant where civil rights leaders have congregated since the early '50s. On the nearby campus of Morris Brown College, students majoring in hospitality administration practice their skills at **Scholars Restaurant** (715 Martin Luther King Jr. Dr., tel. 404/739–1313) in the Hickman Student Center. Daily buffets range from Southern regional to a "seafood extravaganza." (Kids 2 and under eat free.) For something quicker, try pizza at **Papa John's** (10 Northside Dr., tel. 494/524–7272) just around the corner.

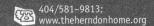

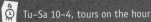
home are various portraits of the Herndons— Alonzo's only child, Norris, appears to have been quite the ham!

Nearly the entire 15-room mansion is accessible during guided tours, but everything is cordoned off with velvet rope and filled with "do not touch" signs, making a visit frustrating for antsy smaller children. Your older kids may appreciate the ornate carved furniture and sparkling chandeliers, but what's really interesting is the guide's narration about all that the Herndons endured through their lives. When Alonzo owned his successful 23-chair barbershop on Peachtree Street, all his barbers were black but all his clients were white. Because of laws at the time, Herndon couldn't even get a haircut in his own shop. Because blacks were forbidden to enter through the front door, Herndon made the back entrance to his shop as beautiful as the front. The shop's original barber pole is on display in the home's lower level.

HEY KIDS! When you're in the front hallway, look at the ferocious carved lions growling on the ends of the banisters at the base of the steps. Then see if you can find similar lions on the edges of the buffet in the dining room.

KEEP IN MIND Parking is very limited around the Herndon Home. If you get there early enough you may be able to find a spot on University Place across the street from the house. If not, your best bet is to turn right immediately past the house onto Walnut Street. Then immediately back up and park on Walnut, a one-way street that runs alongside the house. Pay special attention to the "no parking" signs, as parking is limited to only certain parts of the streets in front and beside the house.

HIGH MUSEUM OF ART

When children meander through the stunning collection of the High Museum of Art, they mostly stroll right by the work of Degas, Monet, and Picasso without a second glance. But when they hit the collection of Howard Finster's folk art on the third floor, their eyes go wide at the sight of all those marbles, those buttons, and all that... well, junk put together to make art. Necks crane to the ceiling—where a lampshade, painted Pringle's can, and cabinet door hang—and then it's over to the telephone pole decorated with tacked-on jewelry, nails, and the occasional LEGO piece. Help the grinning security guards out by keeping little hands from petting the polka-dotted concrete lambs lying down with the colorful stone lion.

Young kids can search for numbers and words in the art works—an old screen door is painted with them and words formed out of marbles are embedded in the big chunks of sidewalk that were once at Finster's house. (For the record, there's at least one

HEY, KIDS!
Check out the Visual Arts Learning Space on the first floor where you can play with magnets, computers, and pencils to study art. Be sure to draw on the wall mural and make a postcard picture. Next time you come, it might be on display.

EATS FOR KIDS The onsite **High Café** (tel. 404/733–4545) prepares fancy, expensive sandwiches that might not be so appealing to kids. However, there's a great selection of cookies and baked goods for snacks. If you're there at lunchtime, the **Barker Hot Dog Cart** parks outside the Memorial Arts building next to the High from about 11 to 2 each day. There's also New York-style pizza-by-the-slice across the street at **Vespucci's** (1389 Peachtree St., tel. 404/733–5500). Grab a burger or sandwich at **Mick's** (2110 Peachtree Rd., tel. 404/351–6425) and sit street-side to watch the bustling crowd on Peachtree.

1280 Peachtree St.,
Woodruff Arts Center, Midtown

$8 adults, $4 ages 6–17

404/733–4400, 404/733–HIGH
recording; www.highmuseum.org

T–Sa 10–5, Su 12–5

3 and up

plastic elephant as well as hundreds of marbles, buttons, nails, and pieces of glass in those couple of feet of concrete.)

Just around the corner is the contemporary art exhibit, where a child can provide interpretations as interesting as any curator's. Children see lizards in the big colorful abstract blobs of paint and proudly proclaim that the 20-foot high canvas in hot pink, black, and blue is just like something they could paint.

While walking down the ramps that wrap around this sleek, all-white building, look out for the "snake man" on the 2nd floor's wall. Really a mural called *New Figuration*, the man with the reptile's body is made of plastic plates, wheels from toy cars, combs, toothbrushes, curlers, and all sorts of plastic jars and lids. Children run from his nose to his toes, entranced. Even Picasso looks boring next to this.

KEEP IN MIND On Toddler Thursdays (Sep–July, 10–3), each adult who brings a child between the ages of 2 and 5 gets free admission. After looking for a specific piece of art in the museum, tots go downstairs to a workshop where they create a masterpiece using that artwork as inspiration. Kids ages 6 to 12 can take part in workshops the first and second Saturday of each month (10 AM and 12 PM; free with museum admission) that include a gallery tour, games, and an art activity.

HISTORIC OAKLAND CEMETERY

A longside an uneven stone walkway at the cemetery is a small stone grave marker topped with a carved little lamb. It's the final resting place for "Tweet," a pet mockingbird who died in 1874. When the bird's owner asked for a headstone shaped like a bird, the carver didn't know how to make one. So he made a lamb instead. While adults prefer to visit the gravesites of *Gone With the Wind* author Margaret Mitchell and golfer Bobby Jones, kids pay their respects to Tweet. Many leave notes and flowers on his long-remembered little grave.

This last stop for legions of Confederate soldiers and blue-blooded Atlanta families doubles as an 88-acre public city park frequented by joggers, dog-walkers, and picnickers. Paths wind through gigantic magnolias guarding intricately carved monuments and fountains. Kids think the mausoleums, like the Austell family's elaborate one with huge iron scrolled doors and four spires, are perfectly sized castles. "I'm a queen," said one little girl, curtsying at the entrance before running off to pick dandelions.

EATS FOR KIDS Half the fun of visiting Oakland Cemetery is spreading out a picnic lunch on a shady spot between the headstones. If that's too creepy for you, there are limited restaurant choices in the neighborhood. Right across the street is **Ria's Bluebird Café** (421 Memorial Dr., tel. 404/521–3737), a small diner that serves breakfast all day and some funky sandwiches. If the weather's nice, sit on the patio. There's also tasty New York pizza by the slice at the bustling **Grant Central Pizza and Pasta** (451 Cherokee Ave., tel. 404/523–8900), less than a half-mile away.

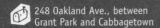 248 Oakland Ave., between
Grant Park and Cabbagetown

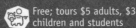 Free; tours $5 adults, $3
children and students

 404/688-2107;
http://oaklandcemetery.com/

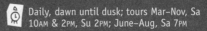 Daily, dawn until dusk; tours Mar–Nov, Sa
10AM & 2PM, Su 2PM; June–Aug, Sa 7PM

 4 and up

Some might question letting children cavort among the gravestones, but the cemetery's preservation organization, the Historic Oakland Foundation, encourages children and families to visit. In addition to the genuine beauty of the many styles of architecture, stained glass, and sculpture, the cemetery can give you a chance to discuss history—the forlorn row upon row of nearly identical markers in the Confederate Section, for example—as well as life and death. For older kids, serious discussions can arise over the separation of African-Americans and Jews or the enormity and sadness of Potter's Field, where some 7,500 nameless Atlantans are said to be buried.

But for younger children, it's Tweet and the massive stone lion in the Confederate Section that make the biggest impression. For these monuments, many children weave a chain of dandelions before skipping off to find another castle.

HEY, KIDS! Look for Jasper Newton Smith. You can't miss him. His full-length statue stands on top of his mausoleum, near the entrance of the cemetery. Smith, who had his statue carved long before he died, said he wanted it to face the cemetery gates so he could always watch what was going on. Rumor has it that the sculptor carved a necktie on the statue and Smith insisted it be chiseled off, because he never wore one in real life.

KEEP IN MIND
You can buy a $2 map at the visitors' center (open M–Sa 9–5, Su 1–5) and take a self-guided stroll through the cemetery. On weekends, there's a 90-minute guided walking tour.

JIMMY CARTER LIBRARY AND MUSEUM

Georgia's most famous political son, former president and Nobel Peace Prize winner Jimmy Carter, has his official presidential library and museum in Atlanta, about 150 miles north of his Plains hometown. The museum covers Carter's life and career, and takes a look at issues faced by the presidency such as war and peace, human rights, and the economy.

If your child dreams of growing up to be president, have her peek into the cases that display memorabilia from Carter's childhood years. There's his 6th grade report card (nearly all A's), his basketball team picture from Plains High School, and one of his 4th grade math tests. An entire room is devoted to Carter's presidential campaigns. It's filled with bumper stickers, lapel buttons, editorial cartoons, and an incredible array of peanut-shaped memorabilia, playing on Carter's first career as a peanut farmer. Little kids get a kick out of the campaign sign showing a peanut devouring an elephant, the peanut necklaces, and the posters of grinning peanuts depicting Carter's famous toothy smile.

KEEP IN MIND If you want to help your child research a history term paper, you can't just visit the Carter Library and start taking notes. It's a lengthy process to even get permission to use the library's vast resources, starting with an initial call, letter, or email.

EATS FOR KIDS Copenhill Café on the museum's lower level serves soup, sandwiches, and desserts. If the weather's good, sit outside next to the pond where huge koi fish live. (They're fed daily at 11:30.) If you visit on a Sunday, try a brunch of berry pancakes, all kinds of omelettes, and Mom's Chocolate Cake down the street at **Babette's Café** (573 N. Highland Ave., tel. 404/523–9121). Also down the block is **Manuel's Tavern** (602 N. Highland Ave., tel. 404/525–3447), a favorite hangout for politicians and reporters and a place where the Carters still occasionally stop in. The pub serves burgers, lasagna, and all kinds of sandwiches.

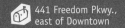

441 Freedom Pkwy.,
east of Downtown

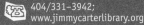

404/331-3942;
www.jimmycarterlibrary.org

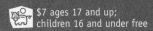

$7 ages 17 and up;
children 16 and under free

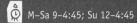

M–Sa 9–4:45; Su 12–4:45

8 and up

You can even get a pretty realistic look at the Oval Office here. The world's most exact replica is complete down to the ashtrays, the view out the window, and "The Buck Stops Here" plaque on the desk. In a recording, Carter talks about his time behind that big imposing desk. Point out to junior high schoolers important documents such as Carter's hand-written notes from the Middle East peace meetings at Camp David, and previously classified memos about the Panama Canal Treaty.

Look for the gifts—like a hand-woven tapestry of George Washington from Iran and a carved elephant tusk from Nigeria—that were presented to Jimmy and Rosalynn Carter from world leaders. They're on display here because presidents aren't permitted to personally keep those gifts. Not even the peanut-shape watch from Mexico.

HEY KIDS! Check out the painting by Mexican artist Octavio Ocampo near the Carter boyhood exhibit. From far away, it looks like a standard portrait of the former president. But when you get close you can see that it's actually made up of tiny images. His left arm, for example, is really a collage of historic buildings from his Plains hometown. The fingers are really semi trucks and cars. His right hand is made of sailboats and ships and his forehead and hair are composed of flags. The painting was a gift to the Carters from the United Mexican States.

KANGAROO CONSERVATION CENTER

I f you take your kids to the Kangaroo Conservation Center hoping to see at least a couple of kangaroos, are you in for a surprise. The Dawsonville farm is home to more than 200, the largest kangaroo collection outside of Australia. During your two-hour tour of the grounds, you're likely to see at least half of them! Spread over 87 acres and surrounded by an 8-foot high fence, the farm is far from tourist-y. There are no signs pointing the way and you have to buzz at the gate to get in. Inside the compound, you're transported into the Australian Outback with aborigine music playing at the barn and boomerang demonstrations underway on the lawn.

But first, everyone is drawn to the fence, awed by kangaroo sightings. A mob of marsupials (yes, that's the official name for a group of kangaroos) rests in the shade under some big oak trees. There's some strange movement in the belly of one lolling kangaroo. Suddenly, a small head emerges as a joey checks out the interesting camera-clicking group. Watch another pouch and there's a single leg and tail protruding!

EATS FOR KIDS The nearest eatery is about four miles away inside the Lodge at Amicalola Falls State Park. The **Maple Restaurant** (Hwy. 52, tel. 706/265–8888) offers daily breakfast, lunch and dinner buffets along with spectacular mountain views. In downtown Dawsonville there's the local family hang-out, the **Dawsonville Pool Room** (101 E 1st St., tel. 706/265–2792) filled with NASCAR memorabilia and known for its made-from-scratch "bully burgers." The **Finish Line Restaurant** (11 Hwy. 9, tel. 706/265–1859) across from the court house offers kid-pleasers such as peanut butter and jelly, grilled cheese sandwiches, and hot dogs.

 222 Bailey Waters Rd.,
Dawsonville

 706/265–6100;
www.kangaroocenter.com

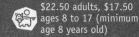 $22.50 adults, $17.50
ages 8 to 17 (minimum
age 8 years old)

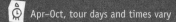 Apr–Oct, tour days and times vary

 8 and up

Everyone is called away from the fence and climbs aboard a converted 1968 army truck equipped with benches. The truck lumbers off through the gate right into the farm's designated outback. The bumpy ride covers some steep, uneven terrain making you feel as if you're really on some type of safari. All around, kangaroos lounge until the truck gets too close. Then they jump—sometimes as far as 30 or 40 feet in a single bound.

After the outback ride, you'll be herded into the barn arena where Rosie (a red kangaroo who sniffs people's shoes), and an assortment of dik-diks (tiny antelopes), spring hares, and other Australian native animals are paraded out for petting and photo opportunities. It's definitely a "g'day."

HEY, KIDS! See if you can watch a joey (baby kangaroo) get back into its mother's pouch. They go in head first, doing a somersault as they go. Sometimes they stick their heads out right away, but often you only see their tail or maybe a leg.

KEEP IN MIND Although younger kids would surely get a kick out of all the kangaroos, the center is open only to children who are at least 8 years old. The owners are concerned that loud kids might scare the timid animals and that the length of the tour might be too much for toddlers to tolerate. In addition, the bumpy truck ride into the farm's outback area can often be a bit harrowing. It's a good idea to keep your kids from sitting on the outside ends of the truck benches. (Or at least hang on tight to them!)

KENNESAW MOUNTAIN NATIONAL BATTLEFIELD PARK

More than just a pretty tract of the woods, Kennesaw Mountain is also a part of Civil War history. Make the visitor's center your first stop, where a short film tells of the battle that raged for two weeks on the mountain in 1864. The Confederate army stopped General Sherman here—at least temporarily—on his march to take Atlanta. At Cheatham Hill you can walk amid the earthen trenches where Confederate soldiers dug in while Sherman's Union soldiers advanced across the open field below. Nearly 3,000 soldiers died here. Some say you can feel their ghosts.

Children too young to be interested in the War Between the States are at least curious about Cheatham Hill's two huge cannons and enjoy the open spaces. The immense lawn outside the visitor's center is a destination in itself. Spread out a blanket and watch your little ones race across the field through the tall grass.

KEEP IN MIND Throughout the summer, the Civil War revisits Kennesaw through all types of living history events such as infantry and artillery demonstrations, guided history walks, and cannon talks and demonstrations. For schedules, call the park or check the Web site.

EATS FOR KIDS Because this is a historic battlefield, there are a few more restrictions than you'd find in a regular park. Picnicking is only permitted in a couple of designated areas including one near the visitor's center and another at the south end of the property. Outside the park, **My Cousin Vinny's** (1220 Cobb Pkwy., tel. 770/423–0312) is a family-style Italian restaurant serving pizza and sandwiches. Nearby Barrett Parkway is lined with dozens of fast-food and other restaurants including **Carrabba's Italian Grill** (1160 Barrett Pkwy., tel. 770/499–0338), whose *bambini* menu offers spaghetti and meatballs, pizza, and chicken fingers.

I-75 exit 269, Kennesaw

 Free

 Daily, dawn to dusk

770/427–4686;
www.nps.gov/kemo

 All ages

Of the more than 16 miles of trails in the 2,884-acre park that are open to hikers and horseback riders, the walk that draws the most first-time visitors is the incredibly scenic one-mile trek up to the top of Kennesaw Mountain. It's paved, but too steep to be stroller-friendly unless you want a strenuous workout. The view, however, is spectacular. You can see as far east as Stone Mountain and as far south as downtown. During the week, you can also drive to the top. On weekends, you have to walk or take the shuttle bus that runs every few minutes (consider taking the bus to the top and hoofing it down).

An interesting footnote is that this beautiful spot of land held the dead even before the Civil War. The Cherokee lived in the area in the early 1800s, and the mountain takes its name from their word for burial ground.

HEY, KIDS! How would you like to be a Junior Ranger? Buy a training guide ($2) in the visitor's center and you're on your way. The book is filled with all kinds of questions about topics like air pollution, geography, and nature. There are also plenty of fun word scrambles and other puzzles about the great outdoors. When you answer all the questions and complete all the puzzles, have your book signed by a ranger. Take the guide back to the visitor's center and you'll get a Junior Ranger badge or pin in exchange for all your work.

LAKE LANIER ISLANDS BEACH & WATERPARK

While many waterparks in the middle of suburbia are just a collection of big plastic slides and swimming pools, Lake Lanier Islands has all that hoopla plus a sparkling blue natural lake, a mile-long beach, and greenery as its backdrop.

Tall-enough older kids rush from slide to slide—with names like Intimidator, Typhoon, and Twister—seeing who can make the biggest splash or scream the loudest. The bravest try to hang ten on a virtual wave simulator that allows surfing on kneeboards. Some ride the waves, others get tossed into the churning (but knee-high) water. (Kids have to be at least 42" to ride most slides; some require them to be at least 48".)

The place to grab lounge chairs if you have children under 6 or 7 years old is the Wiggle Wave area (for those under 48"). Kids climb aboard huge floating crocodiles and lily pads after ducking under Crayon-shaped fountains and slipping down kiddie-sized padded yellow slides.

EATS FOR KIDS Although coolers and glass containers aren't allowed in the waterpark, picnicking is encouraged throughout the grounds. There are tables overlooking the beach, as well as plenty of room on the grass. On the beach side, there's **Papa Coots**, an indoor mini food court selling subs and sandwiches, Pizza Hut individual pizzas, and Edy's ice cream. Over near the wave pool is the **Islands Grill**, which offers kid's meals (burgers, fries, and a drink), served in a colorful plastic sand bucket. There are also concession stands like the **Wacky Quacker Snacky Shacker** selling ice cream and drinks.

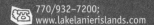
7000 Holiday Rd., on
Lake Lanier near Buford

770/932–7200;
www.lakelanierislands.com

$25.99 adults, $16.99
children under 42", chil-
dren 2 and under free

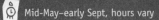
Mid-May–early Sept, hours vary

2 and up

All ages drop into the 800,000-gallon wave pool, which is just mirror-still wading water until the buzzer sounds a warning. That's when the big kids paddle-kick their rafts to the deepest water and the little kids shriek as they brave the low end. The waves start out slow but soon build to an exciting crescendo, scattering rafts and slowly pushing life vest-wearing toddlers back to their parents who sit on beach chairs with their feet in the water. Ten minutes later, all is still again.

While the fake waves are entertaining the masses, real sand beckons from the beach. If you arrive early enough, you can get a spot under one of the gargantuan umbrellas big enough to shade nearly a dozen people.

HEY, KIDS! If you've never gone on a waterslide before, try starting with the Chattahoochee Rapids. You ride on an inner tube (or a double inner tube if you want to ride with a friend). The resulting drop isn't very steep or fast, but it's still fun!

KEEP IN MIND If you want to actually get out on Lake Lanier instead of just wading in the surf, you can rent paddleboats and canoes ($3) at the beach. For a little more excitement, pile into the banana boat—a giant inflatable yellow raft—pulled by a water jet craft ($3, must be 48" tall). There's also free miniature golf near the beach. Outside the waterpark but still on Lake Lanier Islands property you can go trail riding ($25), let the kids take a pony ride ($10), or rent bikes ($5/hour, $12/day).

LAKEWOOD ANTIQUES MARKET

Feel like going on a treasure hunt? Pack up the kids, some cash, and your best bargaining voice and head to the monthly Lakewood Antiques Market at the Lakewood Fairgrounds. Give your kids a couple dollars and send them on a hunt for nifty, inexpensive bric-a-brac that they can find amid the antiques, the collectibles, and the, well, junk.

The laid-back emporium is part flea market, part gold mine. Its 13 acres include seven buildings filled with all kinds of wares from 1950s lunchboxes and Barbie dolls to wrought iron garden accents and high-end antique furniture. But it's hardly boring for the kids. Preschoolers can have a field day looking at all the unusual items like the china dog with the clock in its belly, the towering totem poles, the old Victrolas, and the flying pig statue made from scrap metal. Piles of costume jewelry and racks of vintage clothing set hearts atwitter in little girls who like to play dress-up (and teenage girls

KEEP IN MIND Head to the market dressed for the great outdoors because most of the buildings are neither heated nor air-conditioned. More than half the wares are in the exhibition buildings, the rest are outside.

EATS FOR KIDS Dining at Lakewood is a lot like noshing at a county fair. The food court behind buildings 1 and 2 is lined with the greasy, tasty fare you can only find at festivals. Choose from funnel cakes and mini-donuts, corn dogs and burgers, pizza, and ice cream. There are a few dozen picnic tables, and you're welcome to bring your own food. For sit-down service stop by the **Firehouse Grill** (tel. 404/622–8722) outside the food court, which serves chicken wings, ham and cheese sandwiches, and burgers.

Lakewood Fairgrounds,
2000 Lakewood Ave., Downtown

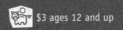 $3 ages 12 and up

Second weekend of every month;
F–Sa 9–6, Su 10–5

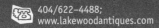404/622–4488;
www.lakewoodantiques.com

 3 and up

looking for vintage style). For the boys, there are boxes packed with Matchbox cars and baseball cards, comic books, and GI Joes. One booth sells nothing but action figures, from Spider-Man and Star Wars to the Teenage Mutant Ninja Turtles and Ghostbusters.

Kids can uncover plenty of inexpensive finds like two dozen marbles for a dollar, children's books for 50 cents, and toys from fast-food fun meals for a quarter. One popular vendor sells pencils, pens, and pencil sharpeners of every type. There's a never-ending rainbow of writing implements, and the most expensive object might be a $2 light-up pen. Most of the buildings have stroller-friendly aisles but beware of the antique china that might be within a baby's reach! If your littlest ones get antsy, a vendor right inside the gate usually has a commercial bubble machine blowing zillions of tiny bubbles out into the crowd. Now that's bargain entertainment.

HEY KIDS! You're not the only ones looking for treasure at Lakewood. Rumor has it that movie star/director Robert Redford (OK, maybe one of his prop people) bought all sorts of stuff here for his movie, *The Legend of Bagger Vance*, which was filmed in nearby Savannah. Even people with lots of money to spend will still bargain with the seller for a lower price —it's known as "haggling." Watch how people offer less money than the dealer is asking for, and see if the price ends up somewhere in between. It's fun to eavesdrop and see who wins!

MARGARET MITCHELL HOUSE & MUSEUM

Any young girl who has swooned over *Gone With the Wind* (the book *or* the movie) should be beside herself when she gets a glimpse into the life of author Margaret Mitchell and the making of her famous book and the resulting film. Mitchell's apartment, her girlhood writings, and props from the movie are part of the hour-long tour.

In the guided tour, you can watch a movie about Mitchell's life, read her diary entries and letters, and see the actual spot in her tiny apartment where she sat at her typewriter and created her massive manuscript. The small sitting room, bedroom, and kitchen are set up with period pieces and replicas of the furniture and accessories that Mitchell used. Older children interested in history—especially the early days of Atlanta and the Civil War—will find a lot to explore through news clippings, photos, and other archives.

But *GWTW* fans will probably be most enthralled by the movie museum. It doesn't have as many costumes and props as the newer *GWTW* Movie Museum in Marietta, but it does have

EATS FOR KIDS There are all sorts of restaurants within easy walking distance. For fun and funky, stroll over to **The Vortex** (878 Peachtree St., tel. 404/875–1667) for award-winning burgers and hot dogs. The odd things hanging from the ceiling (bikes, chairs, wagons, and planes) are guaranteed to give teens more room-decorating ideas. For tasty little "bagellinis" and ice cream, head over to **Orange & Scarlett's** (814 Juniper St., tel. 404/877–0040). Or pack a picnic lunch and spread it on a blanket in nearby Piedmont Park.

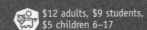

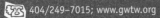
the actual front door to the Tara plantation home and the enormous portrait of Scarlett (clad in royal blue velvet) that hung over the mantle. (Look closely and you may be able to spot the stains where Rhett threw his drink at the portrait.) You'll see original costume sketches as well as Clark Gable's trousers and Vivien Leigh's pink ribboned corset.

Other highlights include foreign-language posters promoting the film, photos and news stories from the movie's 1939 premiere in Atlanta, and pieces of the vase that Scarlett hurled at Rhett. The movie plays constantly on a museum monitor. Between the house and the museum is the gift shop where true buffs can pick up Scarlett dolls, Mammy magnets, and commemorative pencils. It's like taking home a piece of Tara.

KEEP IN MIND

If your kids like what they see, consider signing them up for a summer Creative Writing Camp. Geared for kids ages 9–12, the camp hopes to inspire youngsters within the very walls that Mitchell bounced her ideas off of.

HEY, KIDS! You know how every time a big movie comes out today, stores try to get you to buy toys, books, T-shirts, and prizes at fast food restaurants all related to the movie? Things weren't all that different in Margaret Mitchell's day. Check out all the memorabilia that was sold more than 60 years ago when *Gone With The Wind* first hit the theaters. There's everything from matches and paper dolls to handkerchiefs and neckties, scarves, and board games.

MARTIN LUTHER KING JR. NATIONAL HISTORIC SITE

While the work of Civil Rights leader Martin Luther King Jr. reached all corners of the nation, the tribute to his life remains right here in his hometown. A two-block historic district in the Sweet Auburn neighborhood encompasses the house where King was born and raised, the church where he preached, and The King Center where he is buried and his legacy endures.

Begin at the National Park Service Visitor Center to get an overview of King's life and mission. At the children's interactive exhibit about the history and future of civil rights, one door is emblazoned with the question, "Who can take the lead in ending injustice?" When your child opens the door, he'll most likely be surprised to see himself in a mirror. There are drawers filled with early portents of the crumbling of the color wall in America—like a 1960s TV Guide with Bill Cosby on the cover and the first black Francie doll (Barbie's friend). If your kids have the staying power, they can watch a poignant 30-minute video about King's life.

HEY KIDS!
In the rose garden across the street from Ebenezer Church take some time to read the plaques around the flowers. Many of them are the thoughts of children such as "If roses can bloom when we plant them, let's plant peace." What would you say?

EATS FOR KIDS There's down-home Southern fare like chopped rib-tips and sweet-potato pie right down the road at the well-worn **Ace Barbecue Barn** (30 Bell St., tel. 404/659–6630), known for its authentic BBQ. Less than one-half mile away, the **Sweet Auburn Curb Market** (209 Edgewood Ave., tel. 404/659–1665) is filled with the sights and smells of ethnic groceries like chitterlings, mortadella, mountain oysters, and turnip greens, as well as a food court. If you just want dessert, try **Jake's Ice Creams & Sorbets** (676 Highland Ave., tel. 404/523–1830) for scoops of chocolate peanut butter or brown sugar-vanilla ice cream.

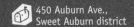 450 Auburn Ave.,
Sweet Auburn district

 Free

 All open Labor Day–Memorial Day, 9–5
daily; Memorial Day–Labor Day, 9–6 daily

 404/331–5190;
www.nps.gov/malu

8 and up

Across the street at The King Center is Freedom Hall (449 Auburn Ave., tel. 404/526–8900) where you can learn about India's proponent of non-violence, Mahatma Gandhi (King's mentor), and Rosa Parks, the ordinary woman who instigated the Montgomery bus boycott. On display are the jean jacket and shoes King wore during his marches, his well-worn Bible, and his 1970 Grammy Award for best spoken word recording, as well as a pair of Ghandi's tiny round-rimmed glasses. Outside in the midst of the reflecting pool is King's marble crypt. Next to it is his eternal flame.

Don't miss the restored Ebenezer Baptist Church (407 Auburn Ave., tel. 404/688–7263) where King preached. His sermons play from the loudspeaker as a steady stream of visitors passes through the small white church adorned with simple stained glass windows. Services take place Sunday at 7:45 AM and 10:45 AM. Down the block is the two-story frame house (501 Auburn Ave.) where King was born (in an upstairs bedroom) and lived until he was 12 years old. It's where he dreamed his earliest dreams.

KEEP IN MIND To receive tickets to tour King's childhood home, be at the visitor center right when it opens at 9 AM. The free tickets are given out on a first-come, first-served basis and it's not unusual for all the day's tours to be filled by 10 AM. You cannot make reservations by phone or in advance for another day. The tours begin on the half-hour from Memorial Day through Labor Day and on the hour the rest of the year. The home has some original furnishings and King's playthings, such as a Lincoln Log set. The headless dolls belonged to King's sister. (He cut their heads off to use as tennis balls!)

MICHAEL C. CARLOS MUSEUM

18

Sometime around age 5 or 6, most little boys get into a gross-out stage. They like to see and hear about icky things—from snakes and other creepy crawlies to ghost stories and skeletons. Those little guys (and often little girls) should be immediately whisked over to the Michael C. Carlos Museum for some personal encounters with some real live (or is that real dead?) mummies.

Follow the twisting curves of the Nile River painted on the ramp to the Ancient Egypt exhibit, where an imposing six-foot stone sarcophagus stands guard. The erect sentinel looks surprisingly friendly, but then he's just a coffin. Past him are ten glass cases—six upright against the walls and four lying on the floor. Inside several are the mummified remains of people from nearly 3,000 years ago—three are *not* hidden by their coffin's top.

Gross, you think. Cool, say the kids as they stare intently into each case. The coffins are intricately decorated pieces of art festooned with elaborate hieroglyphics and drawings of

HEY, KIDS! The ancient Egyptians didn't just mummify people, they also preserved some animals. Look for the mummified remains of snakes, kittens, and even lizards. Sometimes these animals were just pets that the Egyptians loved. When those pets died, their bodies were treated with the same respect as family members. Other mummified animals were creatures such as hawks and falcons that some Egyptians worshipped and thought were holy. Most of the coffins for these mummies are either shaped like the animal inside or have a painting or carving of the animal somewhere on the container.

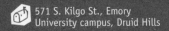
571 S. Kilgo St., Emory
University campus, Druid Hills

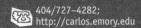
404/727–4282;
http://carlos.emory.edu

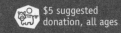
$5 suggested
donation, all ages

Tu–W 10–5, Th 10–9, F–Sa 10–5,
Su 12–5; closed Monday

4 and up

snakes, birds, and half-human, half-animal gods. Each picture, point out the docents, tells a story. Many of the inscriptions are prayers or wishes for the deceased. The mummies themselves are tightly wrapped in much-yellowed linens. Although not exactly the stuff of horror-movie fame, they're definitely human-shaped and a little on the creepy side.

Dozens of tiny amulets that were buried with the dead fill several glass cases. The intricately forged charms elicit a few snickers—especially the ones shaped like "bull men" that remarkably resemble Uncle Fester from *The Addams Family*. Towering on a wall outside the main mummy exhibit is a carving of a glowering Medusa, hair full of snakes. She's as popular with the kids as the various statues throughout the museum that are either headless or missing their bodies. There are plenty of other neat things to see among the museum's 16,000 objects on display. But nothing's as cool as the real corpses.

KEEP IN MIND Ask at the front desk for a free family guide to the Ancient Egypt exhibit. It offers all kinds of "did you know" trivia aimed at kids and sends them on a treasure hunt throughout the exhibit searching for interesting artifacts described in the pamphlet.

EATS FOR KIDS Although the sandwiches and salads at **Caffé Antico** (tel. 404/727–0695) on the museum's third floor might be too frou-frou for many kids, the restaurant does sell tasty brownies and cookies. For more casual fare, walk a couple blocks to **Everybody's Pizza** (1593 N. Decatur Rd., tel. 404/377–7766), a popular college hangout with an eclectic collection of bric-a-brac on the walls. For adventurous little palates, the kid's menu at **Doc Chey's Noodle House** (1556 N. Decatur Rd., tel. 404/378–8188) includes Chinese chicken soup or chicken, carrots, and broccoli over rice.

RAINBOW RANCH

If you'd like to expose your family to fishing but can't spend a whole day idling around a lake waiting for a bite, the Rainbow Ranch is the fishing hole for you. You and your proud fishers will go home with at least a couple of trout in the cooler thanks to the ranch's four ponds overflowing with hungry fish. The ranch promises "guaranteed catch."

You don't have to have a fishing license or even know a thing about casting. Just show up and they'll loan you a fishing pole and a paper cup filled with free earthworms (or corn, for the easily grossed-out). Grab a bucket and a net, then head to the pond of your choice. There are two ponds with fish that average 1½ pounds each, another with fish up to three pounds, and a third with fish that weigh up to a whopping ten pounds. You pay by the pound, so unless you're looking for something to stuff and put on the mantle, consider one of the ponds with the smaller fish.

HEY KIDS!
If you already know how to fish, you can use some of your own equipment at Rainbow Ranch. However, fly rods and artificial lures are not allowed. Just bring your rod by the counter so they can check the line before you head out to the ponds.

KEEP IN MIND Rainbow Ranch is open rain or shine. If showers start, ask to borrow one of the big golf umbrellas stashed behind the counter. Saturday and Sunday mornings are typically the busiest times at the ranch when people jockey for position around the edges of the ponds. The best times to avoid crowds are weekday afternoons. The ranch personnel will clean your fish for an additional 10 percent (plus $1 to bag it in ice). As far as cleaning up your kids, there are two bathrooms on site. They're rustic, but there's plenty of soap and water.

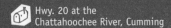
Hwy. 20 at the
Chattahoochee River, Cumming

$3.92/lb., 10% total
cost to clean; $1 to bag
entire catch in ice

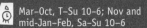
Mar–Oct, T–Su 10–6; Nov and
mid-Jan–Feb, Sa–Su 10–6

770/887–4797;
www.rainbowranchtrout.com

4 and up

If your young fisherfolk have problems getting squirmy worms on their hooks, the ranch's employees are very nice about helping you with the dirty work. Once the worm is dangling, it's nearly instant gratification for the kids who should have a fish within minutes. Be aware that because the fish are so quick to bite, it can make for either a very short—or very expensive—outing.

Fishing at Rainbow Ranch is not for the squeamish. You have to keep whatever you catch. You can't reel in a fish then throw it back in. For some kids—and adults—it's difficult to watch the captured fish thrashing around in the bucket. And, if *that's* hard to witness, don't watch as the employees clean your fish for you!

EATS FOR KIDS You can't get much fresher than what's flopping around in your bucket. If you can't resist dining on your catch, there are a couple of grills on the property that you're welcome to use. You can spread out a blanket on the huge grassy lawn around the ponds and have lunch. If you'd rather put the fish on ice and dine on tacos and burritos, **Pepe's Mexican Grill** (5865 Cumming Hwy., tel. 770/271–1313) is right up the road. Or munch on moo goo gai pan and sweet and sour chicken less than a mile away at **Great China** (5885 Cumming Hwy., tel. 770/614–5566).

RED TOP MOUNTAIN STATE PARK

16

As you and your kids walk through the woods poking sticks at piles of dirt and looking for bugs, listen for rustles in the bushes off the path. It may take a moment, but you're sure to spy a well-camouflaged deer nibbling on some underbrush. Even if the children call out the delight of their discovery, the deer will only look up placidly before slowly walking away. Welcome to Red Top Mountain where the deer are the biggest attraction.

Although the trails are beautiful in their own right, it's the nearly guaranteed white-tail sightings that have earned this state park such a popular reputation. Cars creep slowly on the main drive, fingers and cameras pointed out the window at the does and bucks that graze roadside. The docile creatures—who have actually caused problems for the park because of overpopulation—are just as common on the trails.

A deer sighting is almost as breathtaking as the view at the park's entrance—a bridge that spans sparkling Lake Allatoona. Speedboats and wave-runners zig-zag about as people fish

EATS FOR KIDS The **Mountain Cove Restaurant** (tel. 770/975–0055) in the lodge has a daily breakfast, lunch, and dinner buffet as well as a menu that includes chicken fingers, burgers, and grilled cheese for kids. A seasonal concession stand at the beach sells hot dogs, pretzels, and ice cream. Dozens of picnic tables overlook the lake. There are all sorts of family-friendly spots about 4–5 miles away in Cartersville including **Antonino's Italian Grotto** (28 S. Wall St., tel. 770/387–9664) for spaghetti and pizza and **The Village Porch Cafe** (25 N. Wall St., tel. 770/386–3100) for sandwiches and ice cream.

 I-75 exit 285, Cartersville, on Lake Allatoona

 $2 parking (free on Wednesdays)

 Daily 7 AM–10 PM

 770/975-0055; www.gastateparks.org

All ages

from the shore and dangle their legs in the water. A small, man-made beach is tucked into a pretty cove not far from the Visitors Center. (It's roped off, but there's no lifeguard.)

Of the park's 12 miles of easy-to-moderate hiking trails, the most kid- and stroller-friendly is the Lakeside Trail that starts at the parking lot behind the lodge. The ¾-mile paved path makes a gentle serpentine along the lakeshore and into the woods, going past an 1860s log cabin which occasionally is the site for family-centered programs. The White Tail Trail is a good place for deer encounters. It's fun for kids because it crosses a low, broad wooden bridge from which to spot frogs and fish in the water below. It ends at perhaps the most picturesque spot in the park—a rocky point at the edge of the lake. (Beware, however, that the rocks are incredibly tempting to climb!) Only the deer provide a better photo opportunity.

KEEP IN MIND Family activities abound at Red Top. There are Saturday night bluegrass concerts and story-telling in summer behind the lodge, Halloween hayrides in October, and a Civil War encampment in spring.

HEY, KIDS! You can borrow a fishing pole and a tackle box filled with bait at the Visitors Center for free. Then find a spot on the lake to see if the fish are biting. If you'd rather try your hand at miniature golf, there's a course right next to the beach. You can rent a ball and a club ($3/round) at the beach concession stand in summer or at the Visitors Center the rest of the year.

ROBERT C. WILLIAMS AMERICAN MUSEUM OF PAPERMAKING

While you may get blank stares when you announce a trip this museum, your kids will leave knowing that papermaking is an ancient marriage of art and science, full of ingredients they never would have expected. Kids learn how anything from common vegetables to banana leaves to recycled paper can be broken down and transformed into pulp, and then how various textures, styles, and colors of papers are created.

Part of the Institute of Paper Science and Technology graduate school, the museum is the only papermaking museum *with* a paper collection in the United States. The extensive collection of artifacts includes early Sumerian tablets made in 1934 BC, papyrus legal documents circa the 8th century, printing presses from the 17th century, and a 15-foot-tall wood and metal paper press from the late 18th century. Older kids and teens can read the step-by-step process early papermakers went through— from cutting plants and trees to heavy pounding with wooden mallets and huge stones— and then see the intricate writing and symbols that were engraved on each sheet.

HEY, KIDS!

What do you think is used to make U.S. dollar bills? One of the main ingredients is scraps of fabric left over when blue jeans are made! The denim makes the paper strong so it survives handling and even occasional trips through the washing machine.

KEEP IN MIND If your kids are intrigued by the idea of making their own paper, there are plenty of how-to books in the museum's gift shop. In addition, there are family hands-on papermaking workshops. (Children must be at least 4 years old.) Held on Saturdays, the 2- to 3-hour classes cover topics like holiday paper crafts, making paper with vegetables, and creating collages. The workshops are all beginner level. Pre-registration is required because the classes are small and fill up quickly and all children must be accompanied by an adult. Dates, times, and fees vary so call the museum for details.

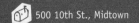 500 10th St., Midtown

 404/894-7840;
www.ipst.edu/amp

 $3 donation ages 3
and up; guided tour,
$3.50 ages 3 and up

 M–F 9–5

 8 and up

Even more fun are oddities like the 1782 lottery ticket and men's paper collars from the 1800s.

Younger kids might enjoy the interactive exhibits including a replica of a papermaking machine. Although no actual paper comes out, the display shows the entire process as wheels turn, motors spin, and engines whir at the push of a button. The whole papermaking procedure is also captured on stereoscope—3D images that kids can watch through special viewers.

Steer your kids toward the museum's large collection of watermarks. In addition to simple names and letters, there are fancy portraits and intricate works of art that are invisible unless you hold them up to the light. Then, like magic, the images appear.

EATS FOR KIDS **The Paper Plate** cafeteria in the lower level of the museum has a small selection of hamburgers and sandwiches, as well as a salad bar and snacks. Right across the street, **Lil Dino Subs** (537 10th St., tel. 404/873–1677) has a vast menu of deli sandwiches ranging from meatball subs to basic ham and cheese. There's also a fair array of cookies and ice cream. In the same strip mall, **City Café Diner** (525 10th St., tel. 404/724–0407) serves the usual sandwiches as well as pancakes and French toast, cheese quesadillas, and Greek gyros.

Atlanta's nationally known science museum does everything but issue lab coats to its young visitors. Understanding the science we see and use in everyday life, from static electricity and energy to robotics and construction, demands 100% hands-on experimentation here. Some of the museum is showing its age, but up through their preteen years, most kids will be too engaged to notice.

Even in this brainy place, kids can show off their brawn in the popular Simple Machines area, the first big area inside the entrance. They'll learn how energy is generated by pedaling long and furiously on a bike, and see just how much energy it takes to power a hair dryer, toaster, or boom box. A lesson in physics proves how even small-fry can effortlessly hoist a 50-pound punching bag (with the help of strategically placed pulleys).

If your child likes creating clever contraptions, point her toward the robotics display at the back of the museum. She can pick a spot at a long table piled with little motors and

KEEP IN MIND There are three programs held each day in the back of the museum in the Science Show Theater (times vary; check the admission desk for details). The shows are nothing fancy (no microphone, lots of yelling) but the kids seem to enjoy them. Try to catch the static electricity demonstration when the host makes a volunteer's hair literally stand on end and shows how bubbles act just like magnets. For younger kids, there's daily face-painting near the Kidspace area at 10:30, 12:30, and 2.

gears and LEGO-like pieces. If the budding engineer puts the pieces together correctly, the robot actually crawls, spins, and creeps over the Mars-like landscape set up around it.

Little kids aren't left out of all the fun. Children under 7 have their own interactive area where they can present the TV news and weather forecasts (while watching themselves on monitors), splash around in a guaranteed-to-soak water play area, and make lots of loud noise in the enclosed music room outfitted with tambourines, maracas, steel drums, and the inner workings of a piano.

All those exploring hands have taken a toll on SciTrek. Some of the exhibits are broken or worn-down, which can be frustrating. Fortunately, there are some 120 permanent exhibits as well as ever-changing temporary displays, so it's unlikely that you'll run out of things to do.

HEY, KIDS! If you like trains, check out SciTrek's electric train exhibit. Two trains chug around 300 feet of track, passing villages and depots. Take the wheel yourself at the computer's train simulator program. You decide where to go, how fast, and when to blow the whistle.

EATS FOR KIDS The only food you can buy at SciTrek comes out of vending machines. The selection is primarily candy bars and snacks but there are microwaves if you want to reheat something from home. About a mile away, you can dine in an old trolley car at **The Old Spaghetti Factory** (249 Ponce de Leon Ave., tel. 404/872–2841), but be prepared for a wait since seating is limited. Plenty of eye-catching decorations—like sparkling chandeliers and fancy old chairs— keep the kids occupied while you wait for heaping bowls of inexpensive spaghetti.

SIX FLAGS OVER GEORGIA

At Six Flags, it's all about the roller coasters. That's where you'll find the longest lines packed with thrill-seeking kids and adults. Sure, there are live shows, bumper cars, and calm rides for the little ones. But the coasters—especially the ones built to test the fearless—are the main attraction.

Of the nine coasters, Superman and Batman are the most popular. Superman, a tangle of red and blue loops and spirals, attempts to make you feel as if you're soaring across the sky just like the superhero on a very turbulent day. (If you're the non-daring type, there are plenty of benches outside the Superman ride. Just be warned: there's no shade!) On the other side of the park in Gotham City, the Batman coaster careens through corkscrews and curves, while you sit in a ski-lift chair, suspended from the track above. Screams from the Caped Crusader's riders intermingle with those from riders right behind them on the MindBender, an incredible triple-loop (two vertical, one horizontal) coaster.

HEY, KIDS!

Besides the safety harness, centrifugal force helps keeps you in your roller coaster seat. A moving object (in this case, your body) wants to keep going in the same direction. So when the coaster loops or goes upside down, your body tries to keep going straight. That force you feel helps keep you in your seat!

KEEP IN MIND
If you *really* abhor waiting in lines, spring for a Q-Bot, a device that lets you queue up in a virtual line. Point your Q-Bot at the kiosk in front of a ride then head off. The gadget beeps when it's your turn to ride. Then you get to jump in a special (and much shorter) line. Unlike the virtual line passes at Disney and Universal parks, the Q-Bot is not free. It's $20 for one person and up to $70 for six people on the same pager. They're rented in a kiosk right inside the park entrance.

 I-20 West, Austell

 770/948-9290;
www.sixflags.com/georgia

 $39.99 over 48",
$24.99 48" and
under

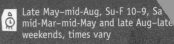 Late May–mid-Aug, Su-F 10–9, Sa
mid-Mar–mid-May and late Aug–late
weekends, times vary

 3 and up

If your kids don't meet the height requirements for the bigger rides there are still plenty of things they can do. Bugs Bunny World has flying swings, planes, and pirate ships, as well as a scaled-down coaster (parents can ride too) and a small arcade.

There are attractions for the whole family such as the Hanson Cars, roadsters on tracks that kids can drive (if accompanied by an adult); the Monster Plantation boat ride (which is mostly fun but is briefly dark and scary); a sky ride across the park; and an old-fashioned horse-filled carousel.

If you want to escape the heat, there are several indoor shows (times vary) and three water rides that nearly guarantee you'll get splashed, if not downright soaked.

EATS FOR KIDS Dozens of food stands and restaurants sell the usual amusement park fare like burgers and corn dogs, frozen lemonade, and funnel cakes. For something different, try **Miss Dixie's Depot** in the Confederate section near the Dahlonega Mine Train. Its Southern buffet features steamed vegetables, turkey legs, corn-on-the-cob, and peach cobbler. The **Miner's CookHouse** outside the Déjà Vu coaster in the Lickskillet section has barbecue pork sandwiches and big juicy slabs of ribs. All the restaurants have kid's meals of some type, ranging from cheeseburgers to chicken nuggets.

THEASTERN RAILWAY MUSEUM

If Thomas the Tank Engine is the love of your child's life, the Southeastern Railway Museum will start his engine running. He'll be craning his neck as soon as you drive through the big metal gates into a rail yard filled with real live diesel engines, cabooses, and passenger cars. The brightest of the bunch is shiny red Georgia Power #97, a little steam locomotive that could be Thomas' half-brother.

Inside a big exhibit building, you can clamber up the metal stairs into a long black 1911 Pullman car draped with red, white and blue bunting. It was President Warren Harding's transportation for his cross-country meet-the-people tour. The seats are remarkably plush, the bathrooms itty-bitty. Wind your way into the attached sleeper car with matchbox-like sleeping compartments jammed with upper and lower berths, original sinks, and even the occasional shower. (Feel free to touch; just don't bounce on the beds.) Even the youngest kids notice how little the beds are!

KEEP IN MIND The Southeastern Railway Museum's gift shop is a treasure trove. In a refurbished train car between the picnic tables and the exhibit hall, the shop is packed with train puzzles, key chains, books, belt buckles, and place mats. There are engineer hats and T-shirts (for adults and kids) as well as locomotive necklaces and picture frames. There's also a fairly hefty selection of *Thomas the Tank Engine* videos, books, and wooden cars, and inexpensive trinkets (pens, erasers, whistles) at the counter.

 3595 Peachtree Rd., off Buford Hwy., Duluth

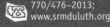 770/476-2013; www.srmduluth.org

 $7 ages 13 and up, $4 ages 2 to 12; train rides $2

 Apr–Nov, Th–Sa 10-5; Dec, Th–Sa 10-4; Jan–Mar, Sa 10-4; some Sun hours

3 and up

The train cars in the building and in the rail yard are hooked together for a maze-like exploration where you can enter and exit at different points along the way. If you have a stroller, forget it. You have to occasionally climb up and down steep metal ladders with not-too-sturdy railings, and the doors between cars are often narrow and definitely not fit for kids-on-wheels. Kids over three should be OK but for younger children, you may want to just admire the outdoor trains from afar.

Train rides run on the hour (on the half hour if there's a big crowd) in restored cabooses pulled by a diesel locomotive. The slow 10- to 15-minute ride backward and forward a couple of times in the rail yard can be anticlimactic. But the big thrill is on the third Saturday of every month when that little red Thomas-like steam engine gets dusted off to pull the train. Then it just doesn't seem to matter how fast or where the train is going!

HEY, KIDS! Did you know that the railroads have always been an important part of Atlanta's history? In fact, when the city was first starting to grow, it was simply known as Terminus (which means "end") because that was the spot where all the southern train routes met.

EATS FOR KIDS Have you ever been in a steak house with mounted animal heads that actually move? That, along with an extensive kids' menu, is the appeal of **Bugaboo Creek Steak House** (3505 Satellite Blvd., tel. 770/476-1500). The fun knickknacks on the wall at **Max & Erma's** (3040 Steve Reynolds Blvd., tel. 770/622-5885) are movie and music related, and kids can't get to the sundae bar soon enough. You can eat a packed lunch at one of the rail yard's picnic tables or drive around the corner to **Shorty Howell Park** (2750 Pleasant Hill Rd., tel. 770/417-2200) where there's a small lake and a playground.

SOUTHFACE ENERGY INSTITUTE

Most children have heard that recycling is important. They help throw newspapers and aluminum cans in the recycling bin, or they've heard lectures about it at school. But Southface—which is an energy-efficient, environmentally-friendly, "green" building— shows many of the ways you can save resources and protect the environment. Terms like "70 percent feldspar flooring" probably don't mean a lot to most kids, but there are plenty of tidbits that might get them thinking about the health of the planet.

On the guided tour, the most intriguing question a staff member poses is, "Can you guess what the downstairs carpeting is made of?" Kids drop to their hands and knees to inspect the dark green speckled surface. When they find out it's plastic—specifically recycled soda pop bottles— all of a sudden the impact of recycling is tangible and pretty darn cool.

HEY, KIDS!
Can you figure out how Southface got its name? The building faces South and that's where the most windows are. That means more light during the day and more heat in the winter. (The awning keeps the building from getting too hot in summer.)

EATS FOR KIDS
Known for all kinds of burgers and chicken sandwiches, **Mick's** (557 Peachtree St., tel. 404/875–6425) has a good-sized kid's menu with all the basics. The big deal though is the big desserts. Kiddie favorites include the Oreo cheese-cake and the monstrous chocolate cream pie. One block away **Great Western Burrito Company** (595 Piedmont Ave., tel. 404/892–1167) has kid's burrito and kid's taco meals that come with a cookie. Get your all-day breakfast at Midtown's **Silver Skillet** (200 14th St., tel. 404/874–1388), a local diner that's always bustling and serves meals quickly.

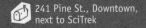 241 Pine St., Downtown, next to SciTrek

404/872–3549; www.southface.org

 Free

 M–F 9–5, Sa 10–5

8 and up

Providing some more fascination are the underground pipes. Kids can see the tops of them and seem visibly impressed when they find out the 200-foot-long pipes go straight down into the ground, capturing the earth's constant 65-degree temp to help warm the house in winter and cool it in summer. Outside, the huge worm-filled composting bins next to the garden draw raves. The garden is completely cared for courtesy of rainwater. Even the littlest kids grasp the concept of using the rainwater instead of turning on the faucet.

But the tour is a lot of talking and not a lot of doing. So, unless your child is incredibly into *This Old House* or saving the environment, Southface might best be visited either before or after a trip to SciTrek next door. Just be prepared after your visit to start collecting rainwater and recycling more at your children's insistence. They'll never look at pop bottles the same way again.

KEEP IN MIND You're welcome to drop by Southface during normal business hours, but it's best to call first to see if a staff member will be on hand to give a tour. If no one is available, pick up a booklet describing a self-guided tour at the front desk. In addition to educating, Southface is an environmental resource center offering consumers, building professionals, and teachers dozens of fact sheets on everything from wall insulation to air conditioning tips. There's also a huge resource library available to members ($50/year for families).

STATE FARMERS MARKET

Even if your children refuse to have any relationship with the vegetables on their plates, those in the stands of the State Farmers Market might at least make them curious. Right off I-75 in Forest Park, the 146-acre Atlanta market is one of the largest in the country, filled with dozens of rows of vendors selling an incredible selection of both usual and exotic fruits and vegetables.

You can drive up and down the streets dividing the stands, but it's more fun to get out and walk. The concrete stalls are a couple of feet off the ground, putting the baskets, barrels and sacks of produce at kids-eye level. The riotous array of colors and shapes goes hand-in-hand with all sorts of interesting, pungent smells.

Items you'll rarely find at the grocery store are unshelled garbanzo beans, Mexican tamarindos, and bundles of sassafras sticks. While some are displayed in little cardboard berry baskets, much of the produce is sold in bulk, since this is where so many restaurants

KEEP IN MIND Although the market stays open round the clock (open every day but Christmas), few vendors are there late at night or early in the morning. The best time to shop is from about 8 AM to 5 PM, when most of the stands are open for business. You'll find the best selection of vegetables from about mid-June through September. The peak time for fruit is usually October through February. Many vendors will offer free samples if you ask, especially when it comes to big, red watermelon in summertime. There's little bartering, and cash is preferred.

 16 Forest Pkwy., Forest Park

 Free

 Daily 24 hours a day

 404/675–1782

2 and up

do their shopping. That means 50-pound yellow sacks of peanuts and purple sacks of pecans that are taller (and heavier) than the average 3-year-old. Monstrous jars of honey come complete with a honeycomb standing in the middle of the sticky nectar. You can even buy actual pickled peppers of Peter Piper fame.

The cultural backgrounds of the vendors are diverse, making for a cacophony of languages, accents, and music. Mexican folk songs blare from a tiny radio at a booth selling corn husks for tamales and bunches of multicolored peppers. Bluegrass wails from the vendor peddling pattypan squash and hot boiled peanuts. Some of the sellers throw their personality into their work. One vendor makes faces out of odd produce that she finds—like the eggplant man with red peppers for lips and tiny potatoes for eyes. Who said vegetables can't be fun?

HEY, KIDS! Take a look above some of the market's stalls. Do you see how some of the booths have rubber snakes hanging from wires suspended above the produce? That's to scare away the nosy birds who try to swoop in and help themselves to lunch!

EATS FOR KIDS Of course you can always load up on fruit and vegetables and eat on the lawn outside the market, but if you want some sit-down fare head to **Thomas Restaurant** (16 Forest Pkwy., tel. 404/361–1367) right on the market grounds. It's a loud, old-fashioned diner serving sandwiches, all-day breakfast, biscuits, and cornbread—all made with fresh ingredients. For Z-burgers and creamy ice cream, steer yourselves less than a mile down the road to **Zesto Drive-In** (151 Forest Pkwy., tel. 404/366–0564).

STONE MOUNTAIN PARK

9

Stone Mountain Park, one of Atlanta's most popular attractions, really does have something for everyone. There's the famous carved granite mountain, a train that rings it, and the skylift that ascends it, a riverboat, and a nightly laser show. But for kids, the biggest thrill is a huge play barn.

The Great Barn may be from the 1870s, but it's more like a giant, four-floor interactive video game. Type your child's name into a computer and strap on a special wristband. Thousands of pieces of fruit (made of foam) rain from the ceiling, getting booted all over the floor as dozens of children scamper around in a frantic attempt to have the biggest harvest. Stuff a mesh bag full of peaches, apples, oranges, and plums and bring your bounty to the kiosks, where you get points in exchange for chores. Put two plums in the fruit chute for 50 points. Move five apples to the harvest machine for 75 points. Put any five fruits in a vacuum for 100 points—then watch them get sucked up a tube

HEY, KIDS!

Have you ever seen liquid glass? Check out the cool glassblowing demonstration in Crossroads where you'll see glass heated to a fiery 2400 degrees! That's about six times hotter than most stoves ever get. The glassblower uses heavy gloves, very long tongs, and even a blowtorch.

EATS FOR KIDS

All the park's restaurants offer kids' meals of some sort. For quick eats, the **Gondola Grill** at the skylift serves burgers and hot dogs and has a great view of the cars heading up, up and away. Near the train depot, **Georgia Railroad Burger Company** has chicken sandwiches, burgers, and fries. For fancier fare and sit-down service, check out **Miss Katie's Sideboard Restaurant** for Southern cooking like chicken and dumplings. Kids get a Moon Pie for dessert with their mac n' cheese, chicken fingers, or burgers. But the fun comes when the servers actually toss the tasty peach rolls to you while you're eating!

 Hwy. 78, Stone Mountain

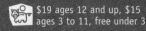 $19 ages 12 and up, $15 ages 3 to 11, free under 3

 770/498-5700; www.stonemountainpark.com

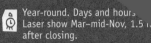 Year-round. Days and hours Laser show Mar–mid-Nov, 1.5 ... after closing.

 2 and up

and thrown across the room into a basket. After each task, swipe your wristband to collect your points. Beware, the wristband scanners are sensitive and can be frustrating when they don't work correctly.

While some kids aim to get their name up on the scoreboard, others climb rope mazes, swoosh down colorful slides, and use huge air guns to blast fruit across the room. It's loud, chaotic, and probably best for kids who are at least four. A couple of enclosed play areas on the first floor are fine for toddlers. There are benches on the main floor for parents who aren't participating but want to *try* to keep an eye on their kids.

If you can tear your kids away from the barn, explore the rest of the 3,200-acre park, including the skylift to the top of the mountain, various museums, and an antebellum plantation. But most of the kid action is at the barn. Watch out for falling peaches!

KEEP IN MIND The skylift is an exhilarating ride up 825 feet to the top of the mountain, providing an up-close look at the Confederate Memorial carving and a panoramic view of metro Atlanta. Surprisingly, more adults than children seem frightened by the 2½-minute cable car journey. (There are restrooms and a snack bar at the top, FYI.) The 4D theater featuring *Tall Tales of the South*, however, might be too much for kids under 5 or 6. The images are surprisingly lifelike as snakes hiss in your face, a skunk really stinks, and rain (lots of real water) comes storming into the theater.

8

Most of the more than 100 friendly animals that live at Tanglewood Farm are kid-sized. From horses and goats to cows, sheep, and pot-bellied pigs, nearly every creature is a miniature breed. And your kids don't have to admire them from afar. They'll have a chance to feed, pet and, in some cases, hold them.

The first stop is the one-room Trading Post, where kids try on cowboy boots and hats, ride a rocking horse, and sit tall in a real saddle while you sign in for the tour that starts from here. Tail-less Manx cats (each named after a country music singer) come running when the tour guide rings a big brass bell. The cats get fed and the guide passes around a bucket so kids can pick out a few slices of fresh wheat bread. The mini pygmy goats, seeing what's going on, start making bleating noises. They're the first to get treats as the kids line up at the fence and start handing out snacks.

EATS FOR KIDS Pack a lunch and eat at the farm's fenced-in picnic area with tables. A swing there is shaped like a bull. A couple miles away, the **Down Home Café** (5060 Sugar Pike Rd., tel. 770/664–2115) promises authentic down-home Southern cooking like fried chicken, steak and gravy, and fried okra. If you'd rather have a more mainstream selection, try the **Corner Café** (11474 Hwy. 20, tel. 770/781–9510) where daily specials run the gamut from beef tips or quesadillas to Philly cheese steak. (There are also burgers, spaghetti, and hot dogs for the more conventional.)

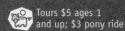
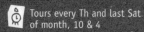
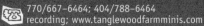

As the feeding finishes at one pen, a ruckus kicks up from the next one—the sheep, cows, and donkeys all know it'll soon be their turn. Kids are invited into the pen filled with gentle babydoll sheep, then are herded into the petting paddock where they can pet and feed everything from chickens and baby goats to ducklings and piglets.

Outside the pens in a gravel arena, kids are told to stand near a barn decorated to resemble a Western town. A guide opens the "Jail" door and month-old Jack Russell terriers are unveiled. They're brought out so the kids can pet them. Then one of the miniature horses in the corral is led out and paraded around for some more hands-on attention. This is one place where you're definitely allowed to feed—and pet—the animals!

KEEP IN MIND
Because kids will be tromping through grass, gravel, mud, and who knows what else, it's a good idea to have them wear sneakers instead of sandals. Besides the fact that they might get dirty, there's the chance they might get stepped on by tiny hooves. If you like what you see, Tanglewood Farm hosts birthday parties (complete with pony rides) either at your house or the farm.

HEY, KIDS! It's fun to be around so many friendly animals, but remember to follow some simple rules. Use quiet voices so the animals aren't scared. Don't run around or leave the group. Feed only the animals that your guide tells you to feed, and then make sure you feed only the wheat bread you're given, not leaves or rocks or that wad of gum from your pocket! Break your bread into tiny pieces for the goats (who have small mouths), but you can give bigger pieces to the sheep, cows, and donkeys. Watch your fingers!

TURNER FIELD

Your kids don't have to last nine innings in their seats to have fun at Turner Field. While the Braves are playing on the diamond, there are plenty of activities off the field to keep young fans entertained. The games begin as soon as you enter the park. Kids up through about age 6 or 7 can toss foam peaches into baskets for prizes while older kids huddle around the handful of free Sega games or make their own baseball cards.

If your kids play Little League, grab a couple tokens ($2) and head for Scouts Alley in left field where they can test their throwing and hitting skills in interactive games. There's face-painting (tomahawks are very popular) for the littlest tykes while serious ball fans can get their fix at kiosks offering trivia and original scouting reports of popular former and current Braves players.

When things get hot, hop on the escalators all the way up to the Coca-Cola Sky Field, dominated by a 38-foot tall Coke bottle constructed of baseball gear. You can walk

HEY KIDS!
See that huge Coke bottle towering over left field? Here's what it's made of: 60 cleats, 48 helmets, 18 catchers' mitts, 86 fielders' gloves, 71 catchers' masks, 290 bats, 24 jerseys, 64 bases, 16 chest protectors, 6,680 balls and lots and lots of bottle caps!

EATS FOR KIDS You're allowed to take your own food and non-alcoholic drinks into Turner Field as long as you carry it in a small cooler and/or plastic grocery bags. There are plenty of eats on site such as 21 types of hot dogs (including bison dogs, chili cheese dogs, and a basic kiddy dog) as well as hand-rolled soft pretzels, ice cream, chicken sandwiches, funnel cakes, and French fries. For sit-down dining there's **The Braves Chop House** (Grand Entry Plaza, tel. 404/614-2437) serving items like Ty Cobb salad, chili burgers, and all-American apple pie.

 755 Hank Aaron Dr., Downtown

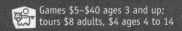 Games $5–$40 ages 3 and up; tours $8 adults, $4 ages 4 to 14

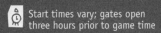 Start times vary; gates open three hours prior to game time

 404/522–7630 info, 404/249–6400 tickets; 404/614–2311 tours; www.atlantabraves.com

 3 and up

under cooling mists while your kids run a base path and sit in a real dugout. Or, for a quiet, air-conditioned time-out, retreat to Tooner Field (in right field), a big room filled with tables and chairs, a snack stand, and monitors televising the game. Up through the seventh inning, the room is visited by Cartoon Network characters such as Scooby-Doo, Yogi Bear, and Fred Flintstone.

Kids old enough to care about the team's history might want to stroll through the Braves Museum & Hall of Fame ($2, ages 7 and up) in left field. The hands-down highlight is a 1954 Pullman passenger car (the Braves' old form of transportation between cities) that you can clamber through.

After Sunday afternoon home games, kids ages 4–14 can actually run the bases. You'll get to accompany them out on the field (a thrill in itself for many parents) but only your kids can do the running!

KEEP IN MIND You don't have to attend a Braves game to get an up-close look at Turner Field. Behind-the-scene tours are conducted daily (M–Sa 9–1, Su 1–3 on non-game days; M–Sa 9–12 game days.) The one-hour tour starts at the Braves Museum & Hall of Fame, then visits to the players' clubhouse (locker room) and dugout, the press box, and the broadcast booth. You'll also see the Coca-Cola Sky Field, Scouts Alley, and a Braves luxury suite.

WHITE WATER ATLANTA

6

On a hot Atlanta day, White Water does its best to turn suburbia into one big beach. There's something for water lovers of all ages—from calm places to splash and float to adrenaline-rush waterslides that provide twists and turns, sheer drops, or just plain speed.

The swim-diaper set waddles through Little Squirt's Island with its friendly turtle spitting streams of water and gentle fountains squirting up from the ground. A smiling tree is rooted in the less than an inch of water that covers the entire playground. If you have only little ones, camp here. There are plenty of chairs and it's close to the restrooms and diaper-changing stations. Let your slightly older—and slightly more adventurous—kids splash around Captain Kid's Cove. They can yank on hanging ropes and let water pour down on their heads. Spinning waterwheels provide a constant rain over small slides and fountains. On Tree House Island, where a huge bucket of water occasionally dumps its cargo on passers-by, they'll figure out dozens of ways to get soaked.

HEY, KIDS! For a real water challenge, head over near the body flumes and activity pool on the right side of the park to try your skill on the Lilypad Crossing. Grab hold of the overhead ropes and try to walk across the water while stepping on floating lily pads and tree trunks. It looks a lot easier than it is because the ropes keep swinging and the lily pads keep moving and bobbing in the water. If you make it across, you have to do the same balance act to make it back. If you slip, you get really wet!

250 Cobb Pkwy.,
Marietta

770/424–9283; www.sixflags.
com/parks/whitewater/home.asp

$29.99 over 48",
$19.99 48" and under

June–mid-Aug, daily 10–8; late May and
mid-Aug–Sept, weekends, times vary

2 and up

For less action-packed adventure, climb aboard the colorful rafts in the Little Hooch River, a slow-moving waterway around the park, or grab some big pink inner tubes and ride the waves in the Atlanta Ocean wave pool. (If you have little ones afraid of the waves, the "ocean" is tranquil every other 15 minutes. Then they can play in the shallow water.) The most family-friendly slide is the Bahama Bob-Slide, a six-person raft ride that zips down a curvy waterway.

If you have both little and older children, head for the right half of the park. That's where daredevils can tackle the biggest, baddest slides while youngsters can play in a nearby activity pool. It's one way you can attempt to keep an eye on all your kids at once. It may not be the beach, but it's cool and wet, and you'll leave without sand in your clothes.

KEEP IN MIND
If you don't want to carry cash around the park, turn in your real money for White Water's Splash Cash. You wear the waterproof wristband and use it for all your purchases. Whatever you don't spend will be refunded to you when you leave.

EATS FOR KIDS You can't bring food or drinks into the park, but there are plenty of places to buy both. Most of the on-site restaurants such as the **Sternwheeler**, **Portside Pizza**, and **Boardwalk Fries** have hot dogs, chicken tenders, and kid's meals featuring peanut butter and jelly sandwiches and soft yogurt. There are also ice cream, soft-frozen lemonade, and funnel cake stands throughout the park. A mile down the road is the famed **Big Chicken** (12 Cobb Pkwy., tel. 770/422–4716), a Kentucky Fried Chicken with a sign shaped like a chicken with rolling eyes and a moving beak.

WILLIAM BREMEN JEWISH HERITAGE MUSEUM

Whether or not you're Jewish, your kids are bound to find the exhibits here fascinating. Historical exhibits and displays of memorabilia and other items—like dreidels and Kiddush cups—bring Jewish culture to vivid life for visitors young and old.

If you're here with a young child, bring her to the front of the Creating Community exhibit. At the elaborate, three-story dollhouse you can make a game out of who can find the items typical of a Jewish home. Amid the tiny ceramic kittens playing in the kitchen and the Ernie and Bert *Sesame Street* dolls on the stairs are an itty-bitty loaf of challah, miniature Hanukkah candles, and a minute Purim *grogger* (noisemaker). A couple of feet away, questions about Judaism are posted on the colorful doors of a cabinet. What is the most important Jewish holiday? Before she immediately throws the door open to find the answer, encourage your child to guess—Passover? Hanukkah? Inside, a vignette depicting a Shabbat dinner reveals the correct answer.

HEY, KIDS!

Ask for a Scavenger Hunt list at the front desk before entering the museum. You'll get a list of all sorts of questions and activities—like "Name three Jewish sports heroes in Atlanta." All you have to do is search through the exhibits to find the answers.

EATS FOR KIDS

Tasty pizza (either by the slice or by the pie) is just a couple of miles away at **Rocky's Brick Oven** (1770 Peachtree St., tel. 404/870–7625). It's a small restaurant with old-fashioned booths and lots of celebrity-patron photos on the walls. But the best part is that the servers will give kids a hunk of pizza dough to play with while they wait. For fare closer to the museum, **Carolyn's Gourmet Café** (1151 W. Peachtree St., tel. 404/607–8100) serves sandwiches, and **The Varsity** (61 North Ave., tel. 404/881–1706) gets big points for its famous burgers and fries.

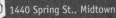 1440 Spring St., Midtown

  M–Th 10–5, F 10–3, Su 1–5

 $5 adults, $3 students, children under 6 free

404/873–1661;
www.atlantajewishmuseum.org

3 and up

Around the corner away from the giggles is the Holocaust gallery. You might want to make sure your pre-teen doesn't wander off alone here, as some of the pictures are very disturbing. Walking past replicas of a Warsaw ghetto wall and a fence that would surround a concentration camp, teens become solemn as they scrutinize hundreds of photos whose images are stark and often horrifying. In a small alcove four computers offer a glimpse into the lives of Holocaust survivors. In the Legacy Project, kids can search by name, country of origin, concentration camp, or ghetto, for profiles of survivors, including poignant oral histories.

The story of the Jewish community in Atlanta from 1845 to the present is the museum's other primary exhibit. A near life-size replica of a Jewish-owned grocery store (called a "mama-papa store") comes complete with empty Coke bottles in the rack out front and a huge jar of peppermint candy on the counter. It's not real, so don't help yourself!

KEEP IN MIND Special programs for children and their families take place throughout the year. Crafts, music, food, and entertainment on Family Fun Days revolve around different themes such as Matzah Madness, when kids get to create "Passover paraphernalia" like napkin rings and Miriam cups. (Free with admission.) "Museum and Me" programs for kids ages 2 to 5 include arts and crafts. ($10 members, $15 nonmembers.) There are also occasional concerts. Call for schedules.

WILLIAM WEINMAN MINERAL MUSEUM

4

ew kids—especially boys—can resist the allure of rocks or dinosaurs. Having both of them in one place makes this museum a haven for wannabe geologists or paleontologists. Although most of the smaller mineral and gemstone specimens are in locked glass cases, there are plenty of big rocks put out to touch. The one that elicits the most intense reactions is a fairly innocuous looking black blob of a stone. A sign asks "What do you think this is?" Kids lift up a small door for the answer, then shriek when they find out, "You just touched fossilized dinosaur poop!" How can something so gross still to be so cool?

In the fossil room, the focus is on "Spike," a replica of a triceratops head. Although he's fake, there are plenty of real dinosaur items scattered about such as bones, fossilized dinosaur tracks, and a real hadrosaur egg along with a CAT scan of the creature inside.

HEY, KIDS! Look for the two oldest specimens in the museum. The oldest fossil is a red, gold, and silver-streaked sleek rock called stromatolite. Scientists estimate it's somewhere around 3.1 billion years old! But the oldest rock in the museum is much, much older than that. The Allende Meteorite looks like an ordinary little black rock. Scientists believe it was formed at the beginning of time when the universe cooled somewhere around 9 to 12 billion years ago (that makes it older than Earth!). It fell from outer space in 1969 and landed in Mexico.

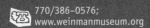 I-75, exit 293, Cartersville

 $4 ages 12 and up,
$3 ages 6 to 11

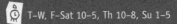 T–W, F–Sat 10–5, Th 10–8, Su 1–5

770/386-0576;
www.weinmanmuseum.org

 3 and up

Nearby, kids use brushes to dust off the sand covering casts of dinosaur fossils. Outside, they dig through big sandboxes for real fossils and pan for gold and gems ($2 per activity) that they can take home.

Amid all the sparkling rocks and hunks of stone in the mineral room is a glass case that holds what looks like a giant brain. The two-foot long pinkish blob from Argentina gets lots of attention for its cranium-like appearance. Although the mineral is technically called rhodochrosite, even the staff members just refer to it as "the brain." But what really draws stares is the boulangerite, a chunk of gray mineral that looks like it's covered in black hair! Many of the girls gather around the birthstone display, marveling at the original forms the stones take before making their way into rings and necklaces. Maybe boys would be more interested in accessories if they were made out of dinosaur bones.

KEEP IN MIND
There are dozens of stones in the museum gift shop that are under $2 including 95-cent snowflake obsidians and deep green adventurines.

EATS FOR KIDS You're welcome to pack your lunch and eat at the picnic tables near the mining equipment and mineral garden. For kid-friendly cuisine, head one exit south where you'll find two local favorites. **Morrell's Restaurant** (75 Hwy. 20, tel. 770/382-1222) is a classic "meat and three" Southern eatery where you pick a meat and three side dishes off the menu. On the other side of the interstate there's **Pruitt's** (5620 Hwy. 20, tel. 770/606-1444), an informal barbecue restaurant that has plenty of outdoor tables for nice-weather dining.

WORLD OF COCA-COLA

Posing underneath a huge revolving Coca-Cola sign, mobs of tourists grin for the camera. The blinking red and white symbol is the world's most recognized trademark and one of the most-visited sites in metro Atlanta, the city where Coke was invented. For kids, however, much of the museum is ho-hum save for the tasting rooms at the end of the museum. That's where it's a free-for-all as kids and adults jockey to get their cups under the dispenser spouts.

Offering samples of American Coke drinks, Tastes of the States makes dispensing fun. Place a cup in the special sensor area and whoosh!—a stream of liquid shoots into the air and magically reappears in your cup. Kids squeal as the beverages take flight over and over to the sound of pulsating music. Although it's constantly being mopped, the floor is perpetually sticky from spilled soda as people switch from drink to drink, sampling the wares of the Coca-Cola empire.

HEY, KIDS!
So, what's Coke made of anyway? You'll never know! The secret recipe is locked away in a bank vault somewhere in downtown Atlanta. Believe it or not, the company has managed to keep the recipe under wraps since the drink was invented back in 1886.

EATS FOR KIDS After filling up on all those free Coke products, you can get lunch right next door at **Johnny Rockets** (50 Upper Alabama St., tel. 404/525–7117) where you can munch on burgers and fries at the fun soda fountain set-up with the 1950s music blasting from the jukebox. Around the corner is **Mick's** (75 Upper Alabama St., tel. 404/525–2825) where the extensive kid's menu—PB&J, grilled cheese, Cheerios— also includes a bowl of ice cream. There are also plenty of options in the food court at **Underground Atlanta** (50 Upper Alabama St.) including **Hot Dog USA** (tel. 404/ 523–5511) and **Villa Pizza** (tel. 404/584–0102).

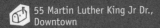55 Martin Luther King Jr Dr.,
Downtown

404/676-5151;
www.woccatlanta.com

$6 ages 12 and up,
$3 children 6–11

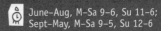June–Aug, M–Sa 9–6, Su 11–6;
Sept–May, M–Sa 9–5, Su 12–6

6 and up

Next door in Tastes of the World, brave drinkers sample concoctions sold outside the U.S. While the drinks hail from as far and wide as Israel, Mozambique, Germany, and Central America, the most kid-friendly drinks come from China and Japan: apricot soda from Japan and the incredibly sweet watermelon drink from China. The libation from Italy is bitter and sure to be immediately spit out by young palates!

Most of the rest of the museum consists of displays of Coke memorabilia such as coupons circa 1896, original Coke bottles, and old Coke calendars. Except for the selection of Coke-themed toys, most aren't that riveting for kids. But wide eyes take in the opening exhibit, a mock set-up of a bottling assembly line where bottles go careening on conveyor belts across the ceiling and up and down the walls.

KEEP IN MIND On the third floor an old-fashioned soda jerk explains how an early glass of Coca-Cola was prepared. Wearing a white hat and a bright red bow tie, the jerk puts on a running show at the counter as visitors ooh and ahh at all the work that went into making one tiny glass. They especially like the part where the carbonated water zips a blast of bubbles into the drink. During it all, there's an authentic old jukebox playing Coke jingles and songs from the early 1900s up through the 1950s.

YELLOW RIVER GAME RANCH

There's nothing fancy about this wildlife mini-zoo, but some 600 animals—from buffalo and raccoons to black bears and bobcats—call these 25 acres home. The deer roam freely along with bold squirrels and lots of birds, while the less hospitable animals (who might eat or be eaten by other animals) are kept behind bars or fences. There are no elaborate re-creations of natural habitats or any other attempts to make this much more than a somewhat exotic petting zoo.

Strings of plain rope keep people from veering off the well-worn dirt and gravel paths. But the shabby edges disappear as soon as a gorgeous doe walks tentatively up to you to take a graham cracker from your hand. She stands still while you gently wrap your arm around her delicate neck and gaze into her big, brown eyes. You can't get that up-close and personal to wildlife anywhere else. That makes Yellow River Game Ranch worth the trip.

EATS FOR KIDS Just up the road is the neon-filled **City Café Diner Restaurant** (1905 Rockbridge Rd., tel. 770/413–6010) where the portions are incredibly huge. The children's menu is filled with the usual grilled cheese, burgers, and chicken fingers, but the best part is the sky-high slices of cake and all sorts of pastries. Nearby is **Frontera Mex-Mex Grill** (5074 Hwy. 78, tel. 770/972–3366) with mini-burritos, soft and crispy tacos, and even cheeseburgers on the menu. There's also plenty of fast food including **Sonic** (4885 Hwy. 78, tel. 770/736–1877) with its kid's meal Wacky Pack that includes a toy gadget.

 4525 Hwy. 78, Lilburn
(near Stone Mountain)

 770/972-6643;
www.yellowrivergameranch.com

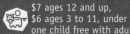 $7 ages 12 and up,
$6 ages 3 to 11, under 3
one child free with adult

 Daily 9:30–6 (last ticket sold at 5)

 2 and up

Clutching 50-cent bags of animal crackers, peanuts, corn, and other feed, little kids take to the trail offering their smorgasbord to any creature they see. The foxes want dog food, while the brazen squirrels and chipmunks prefer peanuts. The animals have quickly learned the best ways to earn snacks. A black bear sits, jaws agape, at the side of her cage willing to sit up and catch animal crackers in her mouth. The Shetland ponies and burros turn their heads sideways and open their mouths so timid children can just drop the corn right in and avoid those scary-looking teeth. They get "real" food along with all the snacks and are smart enough to turn up their noses if they're just not hungry.

Owner Art Rilling says the majority of the ranch's inhabitants were abandoned by owners or found injured or orphaned. It may not be the wild, but all these creatures have found a better life here.

KEEP IN MIND
Although the half-mile dirt and gravel trail that meanders through the ranch is hardly stroller-friendly, for one dollar you can rent a wheeled cart that's strong enough to carry even the most raucous preschooler around the property.

HEY, KIDS! When you're at the game ranch, don't miss a visit to General Beauregard Lee, Georgia's official groundhog. His white mansion sits near the end of the trail, right past the bears. Every Groundhog Day, Georgians are on the edge of their seats waiting to see if Gen. Lee sees his shadow, thereby predicting six more weeks of winter instead of an early spring. Gen. Lee has his own mailbox and there's plenty of paper and pencils inside. You're welcome to write him a letter (and sometimes he even writes back!).

ZOO ATLANTA

Any zoo worth its salt has elephants, giraffes, and a lion or two. But the creatures that make Zoo Atlanta special are the giant pandas and the gorillas, two species that are incredibly captivating to watch. One of only three zoos in the U.S. to house giant pandas, Zoo Atlanta shows off its popular pair in a large habitat where you can watch up close as they munch on bamboo or rest in a hammock. Interactive kiosks show how the panda population has changed worldwide, and a continuously running video details Lun Lun and Yang Yang's 7,526-mile trip from Beijing to Atlanta. Be sure to check out the UPS crate on display that was the pandas' home for the journey.

For another close encounter head to the Ford African Rain Forest, home to nearly two dozen gorillas. The animals live in their natural family groups in four different habitats separated by moats. You can watch them from an outdoor viewing area or go inside and sit in front of the glass in the adjoining conservation center. The decidedly non-self-conscious gorillas come right up to the windows, often toting a baby piggyback style.

KEEP IN MIND Check the information board at the entrance for daily animal demonstrations and feeding times. The gorillas' feedings are at 2 PM and the orangutans' at 2:30 PM daily. To see the animals when they're most active, visit in the morning and late in the afternoon.

EATS FOR KIDS Kids hankering for a hot dog or Philly cheesesteak sandwich will find it at **Nathan's Famous** in the Children's Zoo. There's ice cream at **Ben & Jerry's** outside the elephant house and standard fare at **McDonald's** next to the panda exhibit. Near the gorilla conservation center, **Swahili Market** has pizza, corn dogs, chicken sandwiches, and snacks. There are plenty of tables throughout the zoo if you want to pack your own lunch. Head outside the gate for a picnic in the surrounding historic **Grant Park**, filled with lots of green lawns, stone walls, and benches.

800 Cherokee Ave.,
Grant Park

404/624–5600;
www.zooatlanta.org

$16 ages 12 and up, $11
children ages 3 to 11

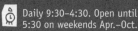
Daily 9:30–4:30. Open until
5:30 on weekends Apr.–Oct.

All ages

Other highlights include the children's zoo, home to massive tortoises that weigh up to 600 pounds as well as a petting zoo where kids can get their hands (gently) on friendly goats and the occasional sheep or potbellied pig.

Rides include a hand-carved carousel where all the animals represented are endangered species, and the train that circles the children's zoo ($1.50 each; $2.50 combo ticket). On the zoo's popular playground, children up to about age 5 or 6 can ride rocking rabbits and turtles and explore an ark complete with steering wheels and binoculars. Visit the playground at the end of the trip instead of the beginning—lest you not be able to tear the kids away to see the animals!

HEY KIDS! How would you like to have a sleepover at the zoo? Pack your sleeping bags and your entire family can spend the night at one of Zoo Atlanta's Night Crawlers family overnight program ($32 members, $35 non-members; must be at least 6 years old). Your slumber party will include a creepy flashlight-tour of the World of Reptiles, which some of the world's most venomous snakes call home. You'll take a nighttime guided trek through the entire zoo when the nocturnal animals are just waking up, and you'll board the train for a midnight ride.

extra! extra!

THE CLASSICS

"I'M THINKING OF AN ANIMAL..." With older kids you can play 20 Questions: Have your leader think of an animal, vegetable, or mineral (or, alternatively, a person, place, or thing) and let everybody else try to guess what it is. The correct guesser takes over as leader. If no one figures out the secret within 20 questions, the first person goes again. With younger children, limit the guessing to animals and don't put a ceiling on how many questions can be asked. With rivalrous siblings, just take turns being leader. Make the game's theme things you expect to see at your day's destination.

"I SEE SOMETHING YOU DON'T SEE AND IT IS BLUE." Stuck for a way to get your youngsters to settle down in a museum? Sit them down on a bench in the middle of a room and play this vintage favorite. The leader gives just one clue—the color—and everybody guesses away.

FUN WITH THE ALPHABET

"I'M GOING TO THE GROCERY..." The first player begins, "I'm going to the grocery and I'm going to buy... " and finishes the sentence with the name of an object, found in grocery stores, that begins with the letter "A". The second player repeats what the first player has said, and adds the name of another item that starts with "B". The third player repeats everything that has been said so far and adds something that begins with "C" and so on through the alphabet. Anyone who skips or misremembers an item is out (or decide up front that you'll give hints to all who need 'em). You can modify the theme depending on where you're going that day, as "I'm going to X and I'm going to see..."

"I'M GOING TO ASIA ON AN ANT TO ACT UP." Working their way through the alphabet, players concoct silly sentences stating where they're going, how they're traveling, and what they'll do.

FAMILY ARK Noah had his ark—here's your chance to build your own. It's easy: Just start naming animals and work your way through the alphabet, from antelope to zebra.

WHAT I SEE, FROM A TO Z In this game, kids look for objects in alphabetical order—first something whose name begins with "A", next an item whose name begins with "B", and so on. If you're in the car, have children do their spotting through their own window. Whoever gets to Z first wins. Or have each child play to beat his own time. Try this one as you make your way through zoos and museums, too.

JUMP-START A CONVERSATION

WHAT IF...? Riding in the car and waiting in a restaurant are great times to get to know your youngsters better. Begin with imaginative questions to prime the pump.

- If you were the tallest man on earth, what would your life be like? The shortest?
- If you had a magic carpet, where would you go? Why? What would you do there?
- If your parents gave you three wishes, what would they be?
- If you were elected president, what changes would you make?
- What animal would you like to be and what would your life be like?
- What's a friend? Who are your best friends? What do you like to do together?
- Describe a day in your life 10 years from now.

DRUTHERS How do your kids really feel about things? Just ask. "Would you rather eat worms or hamburgers? Hamburgers or candy?" Choose serious and silly topics—and have fun!

FAKER, FAKER Reveal three facts about yourself. The catch: One of the facts is a fake. Have your kids ferret out the fiction. Take turns being the faker. Fakers who stump everyone win.

KEEP A STRAIGHT FACE

"HA!" Work your way around the car. First person says "Ha." Second person says "Ha, ha." Third person says "Ha" three times. And so on. Just try to keep a straight face. Or substitute "Here, kitty, kitty, kitty!"

WIGGLE & GIGGLE Give your kids a chance to stick out their tongues at you. Start by making a face, then have the next person imitate you and add a gesture of his own—snapping fingers, winking, clapping, sneezing, or the like. The next person mimics the first two and adds a third gesture, and so on.

JUNIOR OPERA During a designated period of time, have your kids sing everything they want to say.

IGPAY ATINLAY Proclaim the next 30 minutes Pig Latin time, and everybody has to talk in this fun code. To speak it, move the first consonant of every word to the end of the word and add "ay." "Pig" becomes "igpay," and "Latin" becomes "atinlay." To words that being with a vowel, just add "ay" as a suffix.

MORE GOOD TIMES

BUILD A STORY "Once upon a time there lived…" Finish the sentence and ask the rest of your family, one at a time, to add another sentence or two. Bring a tape recorder along to record the narrative—and you can enjoy your creation again and again.

NOT THE GOOFY GAME Have one child name a category. (Some ideas: first names, last names, animals, countries, friends, feelings, foods, hot or cold things, clothing.) Then take turns naming things that fall into that category. You're out if you name something that doesn't belong in the category—or if you can't think of another item to name. When only one person remains, start again. Choose categories depending on where you're going or where you've been—historic topics if you've seen a historic sight, animal topics before or after the zoo, upside-down things if you've been to the circus, and so on. Make the game harder by choosing category items in A-B-C order.

COLOR OF THE DAY Choose a color at the beginning of your outing and have your kids be on the lookout for things that are that color, calling out what they've seen when they spot it. If you want to keep score, keep a running list or use a pen to mark points on your kids' hands for every item they spot.

CLICK If Cam Jansen, the heroine of a popular series of early-reader books, says "Click" as she looks at something, she can remember every detail of what she sees, like a camera (that's how she got her nickname). Say "Click!" Then give each one of your kids a full minute to study a page of a magazine. After everyone has had a turn, go around the car naming items from the page. Players who can't name an item or who make a mistake are out.

THE QUIET GAME Need a good giggle—or a moment of calm to figure out your route? The driver sets a time limit and everybody must be silent. The last person to make a sound wins.

high fives

BEST IN TOWN
Center for Puppetry Arts
Kangaroo Conservation Center
Turner Field
Tanglewood Farm
Crisson Gold Mine

BEST OUTDOORS
Amicalola Falls

BEST MUSEUM
Fernbank Museum of Natural History

BEST CULTURAL ACTIVITY
High Museum of Art

WACKIEST
World of Coca-Cola

NEW & NOTEWORTHY
Gone With the Wind Movie Museum, The Children's Museum of Atlanta
(to open in spring 2003)

SOMETHING FOR EVERYONE

ART ATTACK
Children's Arts Museum, **43**
Funky Chicken Art Project, **35**
High Museum of Art, **27**
Robert C. Williams American Museum of Papermaking, **15**

GOOD SPORTS
Atlanta Rocks!, **52**
Centennial Olympic Park, **47**
ESPN X-Games Skatepark, **38**
Turner Field, **7**

FOOD FIXATION
State Farmers Market, **10**

FARMS & ANIMALS
Burt's Farm, **49**
Cagle's Dairy, **48**
Chateau Élan Winery & Resort, **45**
Georgia International Horse Park, **33**

ALL AROUND TOWN

ELSEWHERE AROUND ATLANTA

MANY THANKS!

To the loves of my life—my husband, John, and my son (and official research assistant), Luke. Writing this book was quite the adventure. Our family rocks!

With love to my mom and dad and my role models, Sophia and Laura. Special thanks to all the kids—Max and Jack, Caleb and Bo, Nicholas and Sierra, Ian and Evelyn, Barrett and Pamela Sue—who helped me discover what's so cool about Atlanta. Finally, thanks to my stellar editor, Christina, for her wit and wisdom.

—Mary Jo DiLonardo

the end!